PATTI SMITH

Tempo
Series Editor: Scott Calhoun

Tempo offers titles that explore rock and popular music through the lens of social and cultural history, revealing the dynamic relationship between musicians, music, and their milieu. Like other major art forms, rock and pop music comment on their cultural, political, and even economic situation, reflecting the technological advances, psychological concerns, religious feelings, and artistic trends of their times. Contributions to the Tempo series are the ideal introduction to major pop and rock artists and genres.

Titles in the Series

PATTI SMITH

America's Punk Rock Rhapsodist

Eric Wendell

ROWMAN & LITTLEFIELD
Lanham • Boulder • New York • London

Published by Rowman & Littlefield
A wholly owned subsidiary of The Rowman & Littlefield Publishing Group,
Inc.
4501 Forbes Boulevard, Suite 200, Lanham, Maryland 20706
www.rowman.com

Unit A, Whitacre Mews, 26-34 Stannery Street, London SE11 4AB, United
Kingdom

British Library Cataloguing in Publication Information Available

Library of Congress Cataloging-in-Publication Data

Wendell, Eric, 1984–.
Patti Smith : America's punk rock rhapsodist / Eric Wendell.
pages cm. — (Tempo : a Rowman & Littlefield music series on rock, pop, and culture)
Includes bibliographical references and index.
ISBN 978-0-8108-8690-2 (cloth : alk. paper) — ISBN 978-0-8108-8691-9 (ebook : alk. paper)
1. Smith, Patti. 2. Rock musicians—United States—Biography. I. Title.
ML420.S672W46 2015
782.42166092—dc23 [B]
2014023315

Printed in the United States of America

CONTENTS

FOREWORD

In the pages that follow is a portrait of the many ways that Patti Smith shook up a baby boomer world by crashing through conventions left and right. What emerged in the wake of her iconoclasm was the creation of the American punk-poet aesthetic and a fresh take on the female pop icon. Smoldering with ideas and arguments, Smith was a red-hot poker forged on the cool streets of New York City. Her form followed the future . . . or might have been from another planet; hers was certainly not the feminine physique that had historically held center stage in American culture.

Speaking of form, later in life Smith would defy conventions again by embracing motherhood and domestic life but on her terms and only after she had successfully, for herself, liberated rock and roll of the male archetype. Smith's sense of style, though, neither indicated nor negated the feminine any more than the masculine. She was an explorer, and she found a welcoming place in an avant-garde community of art and fashion mavericks looking to challenge classical forms, not to mention cultural taste and morality.

Smith absorbed books, poetry, and her parent's Christian religion as a child—sickly, for most of her young years, she had plenty of bedridden time to read—and she released in song and poetry and art what inspired her back into the world, without much regard for the traditional audiences, who for so long relied on a certain stability that all those words and ideas had heretofore provided. She perceived the crucial role that the history of explorers and nonconformers just a few blocks off

Main Street played in the story of any great society. She merged traffic, bringing the energy of America's side street and alleyway cultures onto its thoroughfares.

The tensions between the popular and the radical are often where the most potent critiques of institutional carelessness arise, and Smith seemed right at home in the contradictions that she herself embodied and created. In those tensions, she has made her most effective stands for the agency of the American individual to be whoever she or he wants to be. How one might best know that the iconoclast is actually working to build a better future for her society, rather than just for herself, is by how much care she devotes to creating the new to replace the old. Smith—judging by the quality of her artistic career and the inspiration that she has been to many after her—has cared deeply and has created lovingly.

Scott Calhoun
Series Editor

TIME LINE

American and World Events	Patti Smith Events
December 31, 1946: President Harry Truman officially ends World War II with the signing of Proclamation 2714.	*December 30, 1946:* Patricia Lee Smith is born in Chicago, Illinois.
April 15, 1967: Anti-Vietnam protests occur in New York and San Francisco with more than a half million participating in the protests.	*April 26, 1967:* Gives birth to her first child, which she gives up for adoption.
February 11, 1971: President Nixon signs the Seabed Arms Control Treaty, in an effort to prevent the use of nuclear weapons.	*February 10, 1971:* Performs with Lenny Kaye for the first time at the Poetry Project at St. Mark's Church in New York City.
April 19, 1971: Charles Manson is sentenced to death for the murder of Sharon Tate.	*April 29, 1971:* Smith and playwright Sam Shepard stage their play *Cowboy Mouth* at the American Place Theatre for one night only.
June 25, 1973: Former White House counsel John Dean testifies before the Senate Watergate	*June 1973:* Releases her book of poetry, *Witt*.

American and World Events

Committee regarding his involvement in the Watergate Scandal.

November 27, 1973: U.S. Senate votes 92–3 confirming Gerald Ford as vice president of the United States.

February 4, 1974: Newspaper heiress Patricia Hearst is kidnapped by members of the Symbionese Liberation Army.

June 29, 1974: Soviet dancer Mikhail Baryshnikov defects from the Soviet Union to Canada to seek political asylum.

December 9, 1975: President Gerald Ford signs a $2.3-billion loan authorization for New York City in an effort to prevent financial default.

December 29, 1975: A bomb explosion at LaGuardia Airport in New York City kills eleven.

March 20, 1976: Patti Hearst is convicted of bank robbery.

October 11, 1976: China's "Gang of Four" are arrested, marking a political turn for China.

January 1, 1977: Jacqueline Means becomes the first woman to be ordained an Episcopal priest.

Patti Smith Events

November 1, 1973: Smith and Kaye perform for a Rock 'n' Rimbaud performance, forming the genesis of what would become the Patti Smith Group.

February 1, 1974: The Patti Smith Group begins to perform at CBGB, performing four nights a week for almost two months.

June 1, 1974: Smith records her first two singles "Hey Joe" and "Piss Factory."

December 13, 1975: Horses, Smith's first studio album, is released.

1975: Smith is awarded a Grand Prix Du Disque, the French equivalent of the Grammy, for *Horses.*

March 9, 1976: Smith meets Fred "Sonic" Smith.

October 1976: Radio Ethiopia, Smith's second studio album, is released.

January 23, 1977: During a performance as the opening act for Bob Seger & the Silver Bullet Band, Smith fell off the stage into

American and World Events	Patti Smith Events
	the orchestra pit, resulting in several broken vertebrae in her neck.
March 15, 1978: Somalia and Ethiopia end the Ethiopian-Somali War.	*March 3, 1978: Easter*, Smith's third studio album, is released.
May 4, 1979: Margaret Thatcher is elected the prime minister of England, the first woman to hold the position.	*May 17, 1979: Wave*, Smith's fourth studio album, is released.
September 15, 1979: Stephen M. Lachs is appointed to the Los Angeles County Superior Court, making him the first openly gay judge to be appointed to the position	*September 1, 1979:* Smith retires from the spotlight after performing in Florence, Italy.
November 4, 1979: Three thousand Iranian radicals invade the U.S. embassy in Tehran and take ninety hostages, beginning the Iran Hostage Crisis	*November 1979:* Smith releases the book of poetry *Babel*.
March 21, 1980: President Jimmy Carter announces that the United States will boycott the 1980 Summer Olympics in Moscow due to Russia's occupation of Afghanistan.	*March 1, 1980:* Smith marries Fred "Sonic" Smith in Detroit, Michigan.
March 26, 1982: Ground is broken for the Vietnam Veterans Memorial in Washington, DC.	*1982:* Son Jackson Frederick Smith is born.
June 12, 1987: During a visit to Berlin, President Ronald Reagan asked Soviet Premier Mikhail Gorbachev to "tear down this wall," alluding to the Berlin Wall.	*June 27, 1987:* Daughter Jesse Paris Smith is born.

American and World Events

Patti Smith Events

June 11, 1988: Wembley Stadium in London hosts a concert in celebration of the seventieth birthday of imprisoned African National Congress leader Nelson Mandela.

June 1988: Dream of Life, Smith's fifth studio album, is released.

March 24, 1989: In Alaska's Prince William Sound, the Exxon *Valdez* spills 240,000 barrels of oil, making it one of the largest human-caused environmental disasters in history.

March 9, 1989: Robert Mapplethorpe passes away from complications stemming from AIDS.

June 1, 1990: President George H. W. Bush and Soviet Union leader Mikhail Gorbachev sign a treaty to end production of chemical weapons.

June 3, 1990: Smith's keyboardist Richard Sohl dies of a heart attack.

November 7, 1997: WXYC, the student radio station of the University of North Carolina at Chapel Hill, supplies the world's first Internet radio broadcast.

November 4, 1994: Smith's husband Fred "Sonic" Smith dies of a heart attack at the age of forty-five.

June 15, 1996: A bombing carried out by the Provisional Irish Republican Army injures 212 people in Manchester, England.

June 18, 1996: Gone Again, Smith's sixth studio album, is released.

April 23, 1997: Forty-two villagers are killed in the Omaria massacre in Algeria.

April 5, 1997: Smith's friend poet Allen Ginsberg succumbs to liver cancer at the age of seventy.

September 6, 1997: The funeral of Diana, Princess of Wales, takes place at Westminster Abbey.

September 30, 1997: Peace and Noise, Smith's seventh studio album, is released.

March 12, 2000: Pope John Paul II asks for forgiveness for the sins

March 21, 2000: Gung Ho, Smith's eight studio album, is

American and World Events	*Patti Smith Events*
committed by members of the Catholic Church throughout the church's existence.	released.
March 21, 2002: In Pakistan, Ahmed Omar Saeed Sheikh and three others are charged with the kidnapping and killing of *Wall Street Journal* reporter Daniel Pearl.	*March 19, 2002:* The retrospective album *Land (1975–2002)* is released.
October 24, 2002: Police arrest John Allen Muhammad and Lee Boyd Malvo, ending the Beltway sniper attacks in the area around Washington, DC.	*October 20, 2002:* Smith signed to Columbia Records after spending her career with Arista Records.
February 3, 2003: Record producer Phil Spector is arrested in Los Angeles in relation to the fatal shooting of Lana Clarkson.	*February 7, 2003:* Smith is awarded the Katharine Hepburn Medal from Bryn Mawr College, which recognizes women whose lives, work, and contributions embody the same drive and accomplishments of the four-time-winning actress.
March 19, 2003: The Iraq War begins with the invasion of Iraq by the United States and allied forces.	*2003:* Smith is awarded the Premio Tenco: a lifetime achievement awarded bestowed by the Italian foundation Club Tenco.
April 30, 2004: U.S. media release graphic photos of American soldiers abusing and sexually humiliating Iraqi prisoners at Abu Ghraib prison, leading to a public outcry.	*April 27, 2004: Trampin'*, Smith's ninth studio album, is released.
June 28, 2005: A final design for Manhattan's Freedom Tower,	*June 26, 2005:* Smith curates London's Meltdown Festival,

American and World Events	*Patti Smith Events*
meant to replace the World Trade Center, is formally unveiled.	which features a complete performance of *Horses* in celebration of its release thirty years prior.
July 7, 2005: Four terror attacks occur on the transport network in London, killing fifty-two and injuring more than seven hundred.	*July 10, 2005:* Smith is named a Commander of the Ordre des Arts et des Lettres by the French Minister of Culture.
November 23, 2005: Ellen Johnson-Sirleaf is elected president of Liberia, the first woman to lead an African country.	*November 10, 2005:* Smith is awarded the Women of Valor Award by *ROCKRGRL* magazine.
October 9, 2006: North Korea allegedly tests its first nuclear device, leading to international tension.	*October 15, 2006:* Smith plays at the last night of CBGB, performing a set lasting three and a half hours.
March 9, 2007: The U.S. Department of Justice releases a report finding that the FBI had acted illegally in its use of the Patriot Act to secretly obtain personal information about U.S. citizens.	*March 12, 2007:* Smith is inducted into the Rock and Roll Hall of Fame.
April 16, 2007: The deadliest mass shooting in modern American history occurs at Virginia Polytechnic Institute, where a gunman kills thirty-two people and injures twenty-three others before committing suicide.	*April 17, 2007: Twelve*, Smith's tenth studio album, is released.
May 15, 2008: California becomes the second state to legalize same-sex marriage after the state's own	*May 16, 2008:* Smith receives an honorary doctorate from Rowan University.

American and World Events	*Patti Smith Events*
Supreme Court rules a previous ban unconstitutional.	
January 12, 2010: A 7.0-magnitude earthquake occurs in Haiti, devastating the nation's capital, Port-au-Prince.	*January 19, 2010: Just Kids*, a memoir of Smith's early years in New York City, is released.
May 31, 2010: Nine activists are killed in a clash with soldiers when Israeli naval forces raid and capture a fleet of ships attempting to break the Gaza blockade.	*May 17, 2010:* Smith delivers the commencement address and receives an honorary doctorate from the Pratt Institute at Radio City Music Hall in New York City.
November 28, 2010: WikiLeaks releases more than 250,000 American documents, including 100,000 marked "secret" or "confidential."	*November 17, 2010:* Smith wins the National Book Award for *Just Kids*.
April 27: 2011: In an effort to end an escalating controversy regarding his place of birth, President Obama releases his long-form birth certificate.	*April 21, 2011:* Smith receives the American Society of Composers, Authors, and Publishers Founders Award.
April 29, 2011: Prince William, Duke of Cambridge, marries Kate Middleton at Westminster Abbey.	*April 21, 2011:* Smith is named one of *TIME* magazine's "100 Most Influential People of the Year."
May 1, 2011: U.S. troops and CIA operatives kill Osama bin Laden in Abbottabad, Pakistan.	*May 21, 2011:* Smith delivers the commencement address and receives an honorary doctorate from the School of the Art Institute of Chicago.
August 19, 2011: The West Memphis Three are released from prison after serving eighteen years.	*August 30, 2011:* Smith receives Sweden's "Polar Music Prize," the nation's highest music honor.

American and World Events	Patti Smith Events
June 2, 2012: Former president of Egypt Hosni Mubarak is sentenced to life in prison over allegations of corruption and abuse of bureaucratic power.	*June 1, 2012: Banga,* Smith's eleventh studio album, is released.

ACKNOWLEDGMENTS

I would like to express my gratitude to several people for their help during the writing of this book. I would like to thank Scott Calhoun and Bennett Graff at Rowman & Littlefield for the opportunity to let me dive into a subject that I have wanted to write about for quite some time. Your guidance and patience was a constant source of reward for which I am grateful.

I would like to thank Mitch Blank for his treasure trove of information and insight. Your kind words and help offered much-needed perspective. To every colleague, friend, and library clerk for their assistance, whether big or small, your help proved to be the fuel that kept this project afloat.

To my family, thank you for believing in me and being in my corner throughout this process. And last, I want to thank my girlfriend, Alex, for her humor and grace when I was eyes deep in front of the computer instead of focused on her.

INTRODUCTION

Sophistication, Shock, Subtly

In August 2013, Patti Smith found herself on a most prestigious list. At the age of sixty-six, Smith was included on *Rolling Stone* magazine's list of "The Best Live Acts Now." Nestled between modern progressive rock mainstays Muse and alt-rockers Nick Cave and the Bad Seeds, Smith's inclusion on the list, if nothing else, showed that—even in a musical climate rife with the youthful exuberance of Taylor Swift or Beyoncé or the blue-chip mainstays of the Rolling Stones or Bruce Springsteen—a woman approaching social security age could still shimmy with the rest of them and, arguably, better than she ever has.

But a shout-out from a major music periodical does not a legend make. Smith's inclusion on this list comes from years of cultivating an act that is singularly her own and no one else's. In preparation for this project, my first thought was that it was imperative that I interview Patti. I did not think that this was completely out of the question, as any firsthand accounts and thoughts could serve only to help. Soon after, I realized that maybe this wasn't such a good idea. Smith has been interviewed countless times for countless projects, and I have my doubts that my sleuthing could uncover more information that hasn't already been uncovered. That's not to say that the hypothetical exchange between Smith and me would be fruitless, but as much as this project is about Smith, it is also this author's faithful dedication to an artist.

The first time I heard Smith was as a teenager discovering punk rock in the suburbs of New York City. As a budding historian and musician, I did my research and started with the Ramones, Television, and Blondie. After exhausting those records, I went to my local library and stumbled across the book *Please Kill Me*, by Legs McNeil. The book is an oral history of the punk rock movement through the voices that lived it, including some woman whom I had never heard of named Patti Smith.

I found a corner and began to read the book. I was immediately smitten with Smith. I could tell that she was a real character, someone I should know more about. She was self-deprecating and intelligent, and at that point, I had never heard a note of her music. I immediately went to the CD shelves to find one of her albums. As luck would have it, my usually trustworthy library had only one album: it was entitled *Horses*.

From first glance of the cover, I could tell that she was different. In my mind, she looked like the lovechild of Keith Richards and the witch from the cover of Roald Dahl's *The Witches*—not the most flattering of admissions, I admit, but an honest thought coming from a teenaged boy. I went home and was excited to listen to my new discovery. Until this point, I was used to the three-chord power of the Ramones, the art-rock milieu of the Talking Heads, and the power-pop stylings of Blondie. When I pressed play, I heard the now iconic line "Jesus died for somebody's sins but not mine." This was different; this was important; and that feeling I get from listening to Smith's music has never left me.

A few years later, I was walking along Bleecker Street in Greenwich Village and saw Smith walking on the opposite side of the street. Tall, thin, with long black hair . . . I noticed her right away. My then eighteen-year-old self wanted desperately to say something, but I was too nervous to approach her. I didn't have the guts that day to thank her, but in writing this book, I give her my ultimate thanks.

What pilots this book is not the usual paint-by-numbers approach that other biographies may attempt but rather her music itself. The names and dates, the loves and losses, the points of impact that have helped to shape her music are what's important. Smith's life in the arts is a wholly original design that is equal parts tribute to her influences and her pure artistic creation. In other words . . . less facts, more tracks—let her music do the talking.

The more I listened, the more I reveled in Smith's sophisticated use of the lyric: musical in execution yet poetic on paper. Highly literary, the themes and motives found in her lyrics tell tales of love, religion, and politics. It's been said that lyrics need to be sung and plays need to be performed, but Smith's words usurp any such parameters or media and just need to be.

While artistry can be traced back to primordial elements or influences, Smith's artistry knows no bounds and has helped to shape how we view the twentieth-century female rock star. Smith's creation of a new, androgynous female icon was one of the first to truly fog contemporary society's views of gender, along with her 1970s brethren David Bowie and his glam-rock alter ego Ziggy Stardust, David Johanssen of the New York Dolls, and Roxy Music's Brian Eno.

Although her image was important because it often challenged societal norms, what it communicated was that women were to be taken seriously in an industry run amok with male-driven gravitas and praise. Smith's artistic growth began in the mid- to late 1970s in the vibrant New York City punk rock scene. While this movement birthed its fair share of women, no one commanded and demanded the stage with more individuality than Smith. Colleagues in her court included Blondie lead singer Deborah Harry and Talking Heads bassist Tina Weymouth, but Smith's gung-ho charisma and excellence helped the punk rock movement turn into a universal art form that was heard around the globe. Women in mainstream music during this time were seen as sexual objects first, commercial commodities second, and musicians last. To the record companies at large, a women's talent was always at the bottom of the priority list. Smith would not have any of this.

Smith was brazen and outspoken, and she did not care whether you found her sexy or not—and that, in itself, was in the deep-rooted spirit of punk rock music. This mere idea broke down the convention of the fragile, soft-spoken singer/songwriter and replaced it with a rail-thin middle finger directed right into the heart of the status quo—with an alluring smile to boot.

Following in her footsteps would be a who's who of the alternative music scene, including Sonic Youth's Kim Gordon, Hole's Courtney Love, and a host of other torch wavers who took Smith's ideology and sincerity and broke through the male-dominated posturing of rock and roll. This realization truly came to fruition in the 1990s once the many women then in rock and roll began to speak of how Smith had influenced them. In an interview with *Rolling Stone*, singer Shirley Manson of 1990s alternative group Garbage stated, "I loved how, in her songs, she talked about anything other than the love in her heart for a man. And I loved her image: this non-glam look with the chopped-off hair, looking like a skinny boy." Similarly, Sleater-Kinney and Wild Flag front woman Carrie Brownstein called out in an article for *Esquire* magazine that Smith is "one of the women that every man should listen to" and named "Gloria" one of the best songs of all time, contextualizing it by stating that "her voice is soulful and scary."

That soulful and scary voice of which Brownstein speaks is a determined instrument, one equally adept at rapid-fire poetic verse as well as close-hearted vocal reflection. Smith brought to the forefront the unrefined rock-and-poetry paradigm—which started in the 1960s with the likes of Bob Dylan and Lou Reed—and she delivered it to the anemic Top 40 rock that dominated much of the late 1970s. Upon her debut, Smith's shows contained improvisation, poetry, and rock and roll, all of which were in stark contrast to the New York City rock-and-roll scene at the time. With her debut album, *Horses*, the opinions of Smith were split. There was a section of the public that heralded her as the "grandmother of punk," taking poetry and shining it through the prism of rock and roll. Others thought that she sought to expand the masculine part of herself to sell the public on a strong woman fronting a rock-and-roll band.

But the vulnerability that she displayed onstage eschewed any assumptions that she was hiding behind a masculine persona. Smith's public displays of love, loss, protest, and prophecy reflect less a persona than a personification of the human condition. It is said that the mythologic phoenix rises from the ashes to reclaim its life. Smith not only rose from the ashes of her personal life but used the lessons she learned to nourish a brilliant and exciting career that continues to this day.

And the stage is where Smith appears to be at her most connected to the world. In describing her, Beat luminary William Burroughs said, "Patti came on like a cross between Tristan Tzara and Little Richard, swinging what hips she had, tossing her hair, and singing her poems like there was a Motown beat there, just behind each line."

In an article for the *New York Times Magazine*, authors Tony Hiss and David McClelland likened her performance style to French polymath Antonin Artaud's concept of a "theatre of cruelty," a process where disturbing forms of lighting, sound, and other performance elements are executed to give the audience the most realistic performance style. "She sets up a powerful dramatic tension," they note, "by alternately scaring and eliciting protective feelings from an audience. She aims for the groin and the spine, and as soon as people realize she wants them to like her, they usually do, and things start to cook."

Smith's dynamic interplay of the rock spirit, punk ethos, and poetic prose resulted in the term "rock 'n' Rimbaud," a fitting juxtaposition of her love for rock and roll and the poetry of Arthur Rimbaud. Smith took the now synonymous idea of crafting rock and roll through poetry and amplifier that her precursors Bob Dylan and Jim Morrison tried, and she merged this with politics, religion, and the arts at large. Of all her achievements, the simple act of fusing poetry and rock and roll is her great feat and legacy; it brought the punk rock style and ethos to the forefront. Others have worked at doing the same, but the difference is that Smith has done it better than anyone else.

I

"FOR THE BIBLE TELLS ME SO"

1946–1967

The pursuits of a generation are predicated on what the previous generation encountered and what the next generation has to confront, ultimately setting the stage for future generations and their pursuits. The term "baby boomer" refers to the millions of people who were born post-1945. In musical terms, we could refer to baby boomers as the musicians who were born at the finale of the swing era and the start of the British invasion.

On August 14, 1945, President Harry Truman announced that Japan had surrendered to the Allied Forces, effectively ending World War II, a war that would show its scars on the American people and imprint the weight of war on society. World War II was a chasm in the American psyche, with fears and anxieties on the forefront of modern thought, as well as an overarching sense of patriotism and the economic realities of war.

Music and art emulated patriotic efforts as well as the abstract confusion that wartime can cause. A sampling of art during this time reflects a great deal of what Americans were feeling. Author John Steinbeck's *The Grapes of Wrath* tells the story of the Joad family and its Great Depression–era journey from Oklahoma to California in search of a better life. Director Charlie Chaplin's anti-Nazi film *The Great Dictator* sought to parody the atrocities that German dictator Adolf Hitler was implementing at the time. Composer Aaron Copland's *Fan-*

fare for the Common Man sought its inspiration from vice president Henry A. Wallace's speech "The Century of the Common Man," a speech extolling the value of the work of ordinary citizens in building a great democratic society. This type of world preceded Patti Smith, and she had her work cut out for her for changing it.

Patricia Lee Smith was born on Monday, December 30, 1946, at Grant Hospital on the north side of Chicago, Illinois. Born to Beverly and Grant Smith, Patti came into this world during a blizzard that was assaulting the Chicagoland area at the time. Smith was born a day earlier than scheduled, and her urgency to live and her urgency for experience proved a character trait from the get-go.

Beverly and Grant were your archetypal post–World War II working-class citizens who were slowly spreading their wings after their generation faced the Great Depression and the war. The American environment echoed the postwar notion that wartime fear and anxiety were over and that it was time for America and its citizens to recoup its losses and move forward as a prosperous nation—that the "Keep calm and carry on" notion of life was now a reality and that it was a collective responsibility to move forward.

The arts and contemporary society reflected a need to overcome evil in all its forms. A few days before Smith was born, director Frank Capra's *It's a Wonderful Life* was released. The movie traces the long-standing conflict between a barbarous rich man and a sympathetic, less moneyed family man, which results in a supernatural intervention and an alternate vision of reality. The tale of George Bailey, the less-than-affluent man in question, represents the belief that the will of the common man is regularly threatened by a constant evil, willing to strike at any time. His community—the members of whom recognized that evil was threatening their very core and the values they held close to their hearts—repays Bailey's sacrifices for them, ultimately showing the beauty of their spirits.

Concurrently, America was still trying its best to vanquish any semblance of wartime atrocity with the Nuremberg trials, which sought to bring justice to those afflicted by the Nazi regime. On December 9, 1946, U.S. military courts commenced the prosecution of twenty-three defendants for having been involved in mass murder and atrocities carried out during the Nazi occupation. The trials were successful in bringing justice to those involved and offering a sense of closure to the

American consciousness. As the final earmark of wartime uncertainty, President Truman officially declared on December 31, 1946, that any and all conflict via World War II had ended: one day after Patti was born. Between such beauty and barbarism lay the kernel of Smith's artistic quality.

Although Beverly and Grant were working-class people who did not have a lot of disposable income to expose their children to cultural events, both appreciated the arts and held different artistic pursuits in their lives. Born Beverly Williams on March 19, 1920, to Frank and Marguerite Williams, Beverly was a housewife and a waitress. By Patti's account, Beverly was a capable jazz singer whom she later called a "cigarette tenor." Grant Smith was born on July 29, 1916, and worked the swing shift at the nearby Honeywell factory, a company that manufactured technology for the aerospace and transportation industries. Although a working-class man, he was a tap dancer in his youth as well as a track star. Her father also had an affinity for classical music and Duke Ellington's jazz.

Smith was born sickly and was often plagued with illness throughout her youth. By her father's account, Patti was born with bronchial pneumonia, and he had to keep her alive by holding her over a steaming washtub so that the vapors could clear her bronchi and allow air into her lungs. Smith suffered hallucinations as a child brought on by her illnesses, which often kept her bedridden and isolated as a child. Smith later stated, "I had every single childhood illness—measles, chicken pox, mumps, Asiatic flu, mononucleosis. I was in bed for months with scarlet fever, reading and listening to music."

The Smith family rapidly grew upon the arrival of Patti's sister Linda in 1948. Having Linda in her life proved to be an important component to her emotional stability. In the November 2010 issue of *Oprah* magazine, Smith spoke of Linda as helping her "stay [her] moral course" and as the person to whom she turns when she suffers moral conflict. Smith quickly took to being a big sister, which became all the more important to her with the additional of her brother Todd in 1949. Seeing that their family was outgrowing their Logan Square dwelling, Beverly and Grant packed their kids and migrated to Germantown, Pennsylvania.

Located in northwest Philadelphia, Germantown was a largely German neighborhood, with the Smith family settling into a section of town that housed servicemen and their families. Although the Smith family was not well off financially, they made the best of their lives and sought to have as much fun as possible with what little they had. While living in Germantown, the Smith family often played games together in a empty lot of nearby land they dubbed "The Patch." During the summertime, the adults in the community would sit, talk, and drink wine while the children played.

As a result of being sickly, Smith was skinny, awkward, and conscious of her appearance. As a result, she was forced to put on a defensive veneer to protect herself. Smith created a persona for herself that one could equate to the streetwise toughie found in movies. Speaking to Lisa Robinson in *Hit Parader*, Smith stated, "I had my own gang and everything. I had this eye-patch and kids used to be scared of me because they thought I had an evil eye. I had a cast eye and it used to go up in my head and it was creepy looking."

Beverly instilled in her children the idea of dreaming big and beyond their day-to-day lives. Upon reflecting her mother, Smith stated, "'One day our ship will come in.' If all she had to make for dinner one night was a bag of potatoes, she would say, 'We're going to have a really exciting night tonight,' and she'd make a mountain of french fries. She always made things as positive as possible. She was a big dreamer— when she hit it big she was going to buy a big house by the sea and my brother would have a sports car."

While her home life was less than perfect, Smith found solace in her own counsel, knowing that the apparent awkwardness was temporary and that she was destined for better things. Smith told Victor Bockris, "I was very gawky and homely—real nervous, but I was always happy. I always knew that I was more than what I seemed." In a unique twist, one could surmise that the confidence and bravado that she would later obtain in her performances began as a result of schoolyard bullying. Smith would subdue schoolchildren and their mockery by telling them jokes. Smith contextualized this sentiment with Bockris by stating, "Kids would make fun of me because I was skinny and all that shit, but I would just laugh; I made jokes."

From her formative years, it would appear that Smith always had a visceral relationship with music. While still living in Chicago, Smith recalled the first song that she remembers singing, "Jesus Loves Me," while sitting on a stoop. Written by Anna Bartlett Warner, the popular hymn is a poignant first song for the young Patti to learn, as it originally appeared as a poem in the novel *Say and Seal*, by Susan Warner, mirroring the poem-lyric duality that came to represent Smith's musical output. Around this time, Smith received her first record player, which came with the songs "Tubby the Tuba," by Paul Tripp and George Kleinsinger, and "Big Rock Candy Mountain," by Harry McClintock, which was the first record that she purchased.

Written for narrator and orchestra, "Tubby the Tuba" became a beloved song from Smith's childhood. Released in 1945, the song tells the story of Tubby and his desire to be taken seriously within the orchestra. The song was immensely popular, selling more than eight million copies and introducing many young people to orchestral music. In March 2013, Smith received the opportunity to narrate the song with the Little Orchestra Society at Lincoln Center's Avery Fisher Hall.

"Big Rock Candy Mountain" was Smith's first 45; however, it was not the first single that she purchased. In conversation with Bob Boilen of National Public Radio, Smith said that the first one was "Today's the Day," by singer Maureen Gray. Smith stated, "There were so many singles I loved and wanted, but I loved dancing to that one. So I had bought it so that my siblings and I could dance to it."

At the age of seven, Smith's world was rocked when she discovered the bombastic stylings of Little Richard—in whom she saw a rowdy character who surpassed his contemporaries in both music and likeness. In a world of complicated rock-and-roll idols—such as the wild tornado of Jerry Lee Lewis and the raucous exertions of Chuck Berry—Richards juxtaposed swank, androgyny, and his tough demeanor with a sound that had a profound influence on numerous artists for the next fifty years. Little Richard introduced Smith to a persona that represented the flamboyance and cross-sexuality that stars such as Prince and Lady Gaga would spin into a winning mixture. Speaking to journalist Tom Snyder, Smith said, "To me, Little Richard was a person that was able to focus a certain physical, anarchistic and spiritual energy into a form . . . which we call rock and roll. I heard 'Girl Can't Help It,' I understood it as being something that had to do with my future."

Following the birth of the fourth Smith child, Kimberly, the Smith family was evicted from its home and left Germantown, settling into a ranch house in southern New Jersey, specifically Woodbury Gardens. The family's change from a more urban environment to a suburban life initially threw Smith off her game, as she was weary of her new environment. In the documentary *Dream of Life*, Smith poised, "When I lived in South Jersey, there was no time for daydreams. And life was simpler there. You weren't hassled, people holding you up or trying to goose ya and stuff like that. But that's all there was, there was no chance for extension."

Although life may have been easier in South Jersey, Smith ultimately found her existence there to be constrictive. During this time, Smith began to question the concept of gender within the confines of 1950s suburbia. Smith detested the overly feminine details that were ironed onto women's personalities within society. Smith oftentimes felt disgusted with the classic 1950s-esque vision of women with lipstick and heavy perfume. In contrast to this, Smith saw herself more as the hero of her own story, a Peter Pan–esque character that led a group of merry men. In an interview with *Details* magazine, Smith stated, "All through childhood I resisted the role of a confused skirt tagging the hero. Instead, I was searching for someone crossing the gender boundaries, someone both to be and to be with. I never wanted to be Wendy—I was more like Peter Pan. This was confusing stuff." On one such occasion, Patti, then eleven years old, was approached by her mother for not wearing a shirt in the blazing summer sun. Not understanding that her mother found this inappropriate, Smith was forced to put a shirt on, ultimately feeling a sense of betrayal from her mother, who herself encompassed this 1950s female stereotype.

While the Smith children may have lost the fun that they had with "The Patch" while living in Germantown, in South Jersey they attended performances at Hoedown Hall, a local square-dance hall. Smith reveled in the American folk dance tradition, even stating it as being a "part of me, the fiddler's call." As an adult, Smith purchased the land where Hoedown Hall was located with the intention of keeping it in its natural state but ultimately lost it to eminent domain after a local politician appropriated the land and turned it into soccer fields.

Smith's initial introduction to religion and prayer was influenced by her mother, who taught her a version of Joseph Addison's eighteenth-century children's prayer "Now I Lay Me Down to Sleep." Being an ever-so-precocious child, Smith often had questions that her mother could not answer. To please her young mind, her mother enrolled her in Sunday school, where she learned verses from the Bible and other religious doctrines.

Smith's introduction to religion provided the young girl her first creative outlet, as religion became a major lyrical framework to her compositional output. In her home life, Smith received both ends of the spectrum, as her mother was a practicing Jehovah's Witness and her father an ardent atheist. Although an atheist, Grant was by all accounts an open-minded man who read the Bible and always welcomed a lively debate. "My father was very knowledgeable. He read the Bible several times. He liked to discuss it, he liked to spar, he liked to play devil's advocate."

It was not uncommon for Smith to accompany her mother on Sunday mornings, when they rang doorbells handing out the Jehovah's Witness publications *Watchtowers* and *Awake* to her neighbors. Religion also provided Smith a venue for creative thought and imagination. Smith was troubled by the lines "If I should die before I wake, I pray the Lord my soul to take" and soon began to recite her own prayer and speak from her heart. Smith would oftentimes lie awake at night speaking to God without the confines of prayer or official religious verse. Although one could see how the conflicting religious views could confuse Beverly and Grant's children, above all they tried to instill the concept of being a good person.

Along with her love of prayer, Smith had an equal affinity for literature and the written word. Both her parents shared this love, and it was not uncommon for Smith to sit at the feet of her mother while she smoked and drank coffee with a book on her lap. Smith's father also fueled Smith's hunger for writing. A quiet, distant man, Grant was later described as "part God, part Hagar the Spaceman from Mega City." Even with his eccentric attributes, Grant was always keen on reading, especially the Bible and books about UFOs. Smith's love for the written word extended to a long-standing tradition that Beverly had for Patti, by which she gave her a diary every year for her birthday so that she could begin the new year fresh.

Smith's mother was quick to notice her curiosity and her wanting to read, so she taught her how, beginning with simple children's fables as well as more modern fare, such as the works of Dr. Seuss. "As a little girl I loved books and I learned to read right away and I was reading before I went to school." An early literary favorite was Louisa May Alcott's *Little Women*. In reading the story of four sisters, Smith found a role model in the protagonist, Jo March—a tough, headstrong character who aspires to be a writer. It's easy to see why Smith would gravitate toward Jo, as she has a strong love of literature and writes short stories and even plays for her sisters to perform. Additionally, Jo portrays unconventional behavior for the time, often refusing to adhere to the gender stereotypes that young women were expected to follow, much in the same way that Smith was experiencing at the time.

Smith also found solace in fairy tales such as *The Wizard of Oz* as well as biographies and travel books. Smith later stated, "We didn't have much when we were kids. My parents worked really hard, but we had a happy childhood. And there was always books in our house." Smith's insatiable need to read almost got her in trouble with the authorities when she was eleven years old. During a particularly lean financial period for the family, due to her father being on strike from his job, Smith was helping her mother buy groceries at the local A&P when a copy of the *World Book Encyclopedia* caught her eye. Smith voiced her desire to have it, but her mother said that they did not have the money for it. One day, Smith returned to the A&P alone to fetch milk and bread. Smith began to read the encyclopedia while shopping and couldn't bear to part with it. Smith impulsively put it inside her shirt and tried to walk out the door when the store security guard caught her, releasing her only upon the promise that Smith would tell her mother when she returned home.

At the age of twelve, a family trip to the Museum of Art in Philadelphia changed Patti's perception of art and the circumstances of the human imagination. On this trip, Smith became infatuated with the work of John Singer Sargent, Thomas Eakins, and Pablo Picasso. Smith's father was particularly smitten with the Picasso painting *The Persistence of Memory*, admiring the painter's draftsmanship. With this visit, Smith experienced firsthand the possibilities of art and what the human imagination is capable of producing with materials. "I saw that art existed and after that, it was all I wanted to do."

During her high school years, Smith began to feel the power of music and how it made her feel. One year, a Motown revue came to the Philadelphia airport and the airport drive-in, where for $5 per car the Smith family was able to see the show. Performers included Bennie King, Smoky Robinson, Marvin Gaye, and others. The highlight of the show came when King and Robinson brought a young kid out by the name of Stevie Wonder to perform the song "Fingertips," which caused the entire audience to erupt with applause when he sang "Come on, come on!" Smith later stated that the concert was her "first collective experience" and the power of live music.

A career in the arts was becoming more of a certainty for the young child. However, a career in the arts proved to be a difficult decision in regard to Smith's faith. One of the axioms of being a Jehovah's Witness is that artistic expression of any kind is strictly forbidden. For the religious doctrines in which Beverly believed, it's surprising that she was the one to introduce the young child to music. Once a singer herself, Beverly introduced Patti to vocal jazz singers such as Chris Connor and June Christy as well as operas by Puccini. It was during her teenage years that Smith began to feel the urge to perform. In conversation with Neal Conan of National Public Radio, Smith stated, "When I was a teenager, I dreamed of being an opera singer like Maris Sollis or a jazz singer like June Christie or Chris Connor, approaching songs with the kind of mystical lethargy of Billie Holiday."

Further salvation came in the form of rock and roll—in which Smith found the freewheeling artistic aesthetic that eventually became her performing persona. The Smith children spent their nights listening to rock and roll while their parents worked. It was not uncommon for them to dance to rock music by James Brown, the Shirelles, and Hank Ballard and the Midnighters. Some of the first records that Smith ever purchased were *Shrimp Boats*, by Harry Belafonte; *The Money Tree*, by Patience and Prudence; and *Climb Up*, by Neil Sedaka.

When Smith was having a particular tough illness, Beverly often tried to help her feel better by purchasing her records. Among those were John Coltrane's *My Favorite Things* and Bob Dylan's *Another Side of Bob Dylan*. Perhaps in a foreshadowing event of the power that an album cover can contain—much in the way that *Horses* would be for many—Beverly bought *Another Side of Bob Dylan* because of the cover, telling Patti, "I never heard of the fellow but he looks like somebody you'd like."

Having a particular distaste for the white-bread cultural aesthetic of the time, Smith was drawn to arts that came out of African American communities. Smith told Lisa Robinson of *Hit Parader*, "I never really liked the white stuff, it embarrassed me. I hated the look of the 1950s. . . . Girls would wear big crinolines and lipstick and I thought it was so dumb. I didn't want to be a girl because they wore those Elvis charm bracelets and I couldn't get into that. I had a complete Davy Crockett outfit, I was a relentless tomboy." This may have been due in part to her friends at the time in South Jersey, who were primarily black. Smith stated, "We were really into jazz and poetry and developing our cool and our walk. It was the best education I ever had."

The summer of her sixteenth year, Smith began working in a factory where she inspected handlebars for tricycles. Oftentimes, Smith would escape into her imagination to escape the hold of blue-collar work. Smith's sixteenth year also provided her with one of the greatest revelations that she would experience; she first read the words of Arthur Rimbaud after obtaining a copy of the author's poetry collection *Illuminations* from a bus depot station in Philadelphia. The collection's themes made their way into a lot of Smith's later work, with protest, life, and death making it known. In Rimbaud, Smith found an idol of yesterday that could feed her artistic future.

However much the wallflower Smith described herself as, she was involved in many activities at Deptford Township High School, including stints on the Bulletin Board Committee, the Football Program Committee, the Dance Committee, and chorus. In her senior yearbook photo, Smith listed her life's ambition as being an "art teacher." Although she began to physically take on the personas of Dylan and Rimbaud, her nickname in high school was "Natasha" because her long black hair resembled the character Natasha from the *Rocky and Bullwinkle* program. Additionally, Smith was elected "class clown," which she later described as more a defense mechanism if anything else. Smith contextualized this by stating, "I developed a kind of humor to compensate for being different than everybody."

Early childhood performing heroes came from literary and musical figures but also included the late-night charisma that came from Johnny Carson. "The best thing I learned from Johnny Carson [was] an ability to improvise and to spar." Smith later stated as a teenager that she envisioned herself as his successor. "He didn't just do stuff that people had written for him. And I learned from him. I wanted to be Johnny Carson's successor—that's what I dreamed of. Not of being the next Jim Morrison."

During her early performance experiences, Smith pulled inspiration from Carson, whose loose demeanor and fearless attitude was something that Smith strived to achieve. Smith stated, "When I started performing, I was not well loved. I always pulled from Johnny 'cause he's like a human parachute. He can bail out of any situation and I was always able to one-line them [the audience] to shut these guys up."

After completing her high school studies, Smith enrolled at Glassboro State Teachers College, where she majored in art. Although attending Glassboro as an art major, Smith received early experience onstage as an actress, performing in several plays, including the role of Phaedra in Euripides's *Hippolytus* and Madame Dubonnet in *The Boyfriend*. Smith augmented her studies at Glassboro at the Philadelphia Museum of Art, where she won a scholarship to attend its Saturday morning classes.

Smith did not see a rock-and-roll band until 1965, when she saw the Rolling Stones in an auditorium in New Jersey. "That's the first time I actually saw in person a rock-and-roll band playing instruments." Given the history, Smith's attendance was most likely on November 7, 1965, at Newark Symphony Hall in Newark, New Jersey. An early vocal influence for Smith came courtesy of singer Hank Williams. Speaking to Bob Boilen, Smith stated, "I recognize some of my vocal style, where it came from because there are certain ways that I sing. Being from South Jersey we have sort of a drawl, you know a twang and I listen to him a lot and sang along with him and sing in the same key. He was an influence on me."

The summer of 1966, between her sophomore and junior years, Smith became pregnant with her first child. The father was a local boy, who left her to deal with the problem alone. Deciding that abortion would be too dangerous, Patti served the full term of the pregnancy. Surprisingly, Smith's parents were supportive of their daughter's decision. Given the time frame in which this occurred, it speaks volumes about her parents that they would be as supportive of their daughter, as a pregnant young unmarried woman was frowned upon in society. On Thanksgiving 1966, Smith decided to give the child up for adoption; her professor, Dr. Flick, found a couple who would take the child in. This period of isolation caused Patti to look at her body in a way that she had never had to do so in her life. The already fragile perception that she had of her body increased as she felt the growth of her child alter her appearance.

Smith's parents drove her to a hospital in Camden, where she was ridiculed for her appearance and treated harshly by the nurses on call owing to her status as an unwed woman. Smith's labor was not without difficulty, as her doctor informed her that she was having a breech birth, adding further anxiety. On April 26, 1967, Smith gave birth to her first child, a daughter. Smith later found solace in her postpartum depression by listening to the Rolling Stones.

Smith recalled, "Though I never questioned my decision to give my child up for adoption, I learned that to give life and walk away was not so easy." Furthermore, Smith told Terry Gross on *Fresh Air*, "It would've been difficult for everyone, I think, and the child would have had no father. I felt that I just wasn't ready as a human being, I wasn't prepared and that although I knew that I would be responsible and loving that I just was not equipped to embark on that path."

The memory of her daughter never left her side. In a *Circus* magazine article from December 14, 1976, Smith noted whom she wanted to play her in a movie based on her life story: "My daughter. I have a daughter who's 11 years old. Maybe she'll grow up independent and really really heavy and become a movie star and she'll play me in my life story. She'll be doin' the movie and then, all of a sudden, it'll hit her—I'm her mother. She'll go through all the records and through the whole process of doin' the movie and she'll be startin' to search for me. Then she'll come to this heavy realization about the mother she never knew. This will be after I've had my opium OD."

Following the birth of her child, Smith dropped out of college, partly because the institution left her uninspired and partly because she could not pass biology or the higher mathematics classes. Smith soon found a temporary job at a textbook factory in Philadelphia. The work environment was harsh at best, with her fellow female coworkers harassing her and suspecting her of being a communist after seeing her with her copy of *Illuminations*.

With heartbreak on her breath and the heavy burden of a tactless life in South Jersey, Smith decided that only one place could soothe her soul . . . New York City.

2

"FREE MONEY"

1967–1974

New York City in the 1960s was a city in transition. Ginsberg had already howled; John Coltrane and Miles Davis had painted the town their shades of blue; and composers Philip Glass and Steve Reich sowed the seeds of a brand-new school of compositional thought. Sex and politics were at the forefront of the city's consciousness, with the Stonewall riots demonstrating that oppression of sexual preference would not be tolerated, nor would the ignorance of a government that chose to persecute those of a different sexual preference. New York City represented a rebirth, a prime directive that inspires new arrivals to stand tall with chins up and make something of themselves. This was the call to action to which Patti Smith responded.

Smith's opportunity to escape the confines of South Jersey almost didn't happen. On Monday, July 3, 1967, Smith walked from her house to Woodbury, New Jersey, to catch the bus to Philadelphia, where she would make a connection to Port Authority. Smith's plans soon hit a roadblock when she found out that the fare to New York had more than doubled from what she originally thought it was going to be. Not having enough money and feeling dejected, Smith went to a nearby phone booth and mulled over her options. As luck would have it—or, one might say, as destiny would have—there in the booth located on a shelf was a white purse containing $32 in cash. Against her better judgment,

Smith took the money and purchased her ticket—her freedom to New York City.

Upon her arrival, Smith took the subway to Brooklyn in hopes that she would crash with a few friends who were studying at the nearby Pratt Institute. Unfortunately, they had changed their address, leaving Smith without a place to stay. Smith spent the next several weeks walking around the city, soaking in its glory and dreaming of her new life as it unfolded around her.

Not unlike the sentimental notion of the artists who would come before and after her, Smith's view of New York City was of the romantic location of which Fitzgerald and Whitman spoke. The hopeful place of wonder found its way into writer Dorothy Parker's world and composer George Gershwin's notes. Smith was all too aware of the duality that New York could offer to someone new to town. Speaking to Penny Green for *Interview* in 1973, Smith was quick to point out that although she found acceptance in New York—where her awkward appearance was acknowledged alongside her romantic views—she felt at the time that "New York is bad for me." A mere two years later, Smith sang a different tune when she told *Mademoiselle* magazine, "When I came to New York, I learned that nothing is impossible. I love New York, ya know?"

While Smith was balancing the love that she felt for her new home, the United States was experiencing a social upheaval that continued to spread. In July 1967 alone, more than 159 race riots caused civil unrest in several cities, including Chicago, New York, Milwaukee, and Detroit, the last of which being known as the "12th Street Riot," resulting in 43 deaths, 1,189 injured, more than 7,200 arrests, and more than 2,000 buildings destroyed.

Juxtaposed with the brutality of national race riots was the "Summer of Love" movement, which saw the youth culture of the United States build a social counterculture that sought to fight for gender equality and experiment with drugs and the nation's perception of the young adult population. Alongside this, music was experiencing several highs and lows, with John Coltrane passing away and Jimi Hendrix performing his now infamous set at the Monterey Pop Festival. Not unlike the United States into which Smith was born, people were experiencing the ups and downs of a modern society trying its best to expand on cultural mores . . . or trying to have as much fun as possible while it all burned.

It was also the summer that Smith found one of the true loves of her life, a young artist by the name of Mapplethorpe.

Robert Michael Mapplethorpe was born the third of six children on November 4, 1946, in Hollis, Queens. A few years later, Mapplethorpe's family moved to Floral Park, Queens, a working-class neighborhood situated on the border of Nassau County. Similar to Smith, Mapplethorpe was raised Catholic, attending Christian doctrine classes as part of a well-rounded Catholic upbringing. In 1963, Mapplethorpe began his secondary education at the Pratt Institute, where he studied several art disciplines, including drawing, painting, and sculpture. Mapplethorpe finally found his true voice in photography, particularly when he acquired a Polaroid camera in 1970.

Smith met Mapplethorpe at what should have been her friend's apartment near Pratt, as Mapplethorpe was one of the inhabitants. They met again at Brentano's Bookstore, where Smith was working at the time selling jewelry (she sold him a Persian necklace). Their fates would be sealed one night while Smith was on a date with a patron she met at Brentano's, a date she took only because it promised a hot meal. While strolling through Tompkins Square Park with her date, Smith spotted Mapplethorpe and asked him to pretend to be her boyfriend, to get her out of her date. After that night, the two were inseparable.

For a period of time, Mapplethorpe worked as an usher at the famed Fillmore East, which was a new concert venue in New York City. In March 1968, Mapplethorpe gave Smith a pass to see the Doors. Seeing Jim Morrison onstage provided Smith with a bit of fuel for her future career as a singer. In her memoir *Just Kids*, Smith mentions how she felt a certain kinship with Morrison: "I felt, watching Jim Morrison, that I could do that. I can't say why I thought this. I had nothing in my experience to make he think that would ever be possible, yet I harbored that conceit."

Shortly after, Smith saved enough money to fund a trip to Paris. Taking her sister Linda along for the trip, Smith saw the city that had come to inspire her role models. Smith began to find inspiration within the city while trying to explore its vast terrains, which until then were only figments of her imagination. The city also offered her a way of synthesizing her love for rock and roll with her love of poetry. While in Paris, Smith wished to attend a free concert that the Rolling Stones were throwing in Hyde Park for more than 250,000 attendees in honor of the recent death of their guitarist Brian Jones. Feeling overwhelmed by the loss, Smith began to write poems in his honor in what she would call "for the first time expressing my love for rock and roll within my own work." While small, this event marked a critical juncture in her work, as rock and roll was now a conscious device within her work.

The subsequent year of 1969 proved to be an important year in popular culture. The Woodstock Festival aimed to thread the idealist views of the 1960s counterculture with a three-day event in upstate New York where the world would watch a who's who of popular music take the stage. Adversely, the West Coast equivalent—the Altamont Festival in California—tarnished this idealistic view, causing the youth of the time to become disenchanted and horrified as their generation sunk deeper into wartime malaise. This was an important time for Patti, as it was when she and Mapplethorpe moved into the Chelsea Hotel.

Located on the south side of West 23rd street between 8th and 9th Avenue, the hotel housed artists and thinkers alike. Everyone from Bob Dylan to Arthur Miller to Iggy Pop loitered the halls of the establishment during its heyday. Even composer George Kleinsinger, who wrote Smith's childhood favorite "Tubby the Tuba," had a room at the hotel, a room that he shared with a den of reptiles, including a turtle, a twelve-foot python, a pet alligator, and his twenty-something-year-old girl-friend.

The Chelsea proved to be a most inspiring place for Smith, who reveled in its rich history and colorful clientele. Although Smith and Mapplethorpe were both poor and living penny to penny, their time at the Chelsea proved to be crucial in Smith's development as an artist. The halls of the hotel had been witness to many artists whom Smith held close, including Oscar Wilde, Allen Ginsberg, and William Burroughs. The artistic output of the hotel was so prolific that Smith once referred to it as "my new university."

Opportunities to perform came not from music or poetry but from acting. The playwright Jackie Curtis invited Smith to be a member of the ensemble for her play *Femme Fatale*, where she played a role that was originated for actor John Christian, who refused it after getting addicted to heroin and becoming agoraphobic. The title of the play was taken from the Velvet Underground song of the same name from its debut album, *The Velvet Underground & Nico*. According to Smith's costar Jayne-Wayne County, Smith played an Italian man who was a

member of the mafia. Part of the play included Smith grabbing a hold
of her "penis" and stating in a faux Italian accent "Coma hea, mamma
mia I wanna fucka you with my big ole dickaroo." Additionally, her
character shot up heroin onstage, which Smith did by laying a putty-like
substance on her arm and putting a real needle into it. Smith found
acting to be more of a pain than a pleasure, as she hated the idea of
memorizing dialogue and wearing makeup.

Smith continued to write poetry even though Robert remarked that
she should sing. Smith received a push of sorts one day while waiting
for Robert in the lobby of the Chelsea Hotel. While working on a piece
in her notebook, a stranger asked her what she was doing. She looked
up and saw the face of none other than Bob Neuwirth, the musician and
record producer who was closely associated with Bob Dylan. Neuwirth
took a liking to Smith and invited her to the El Quijote, the bar adjacent
to the hotel. While drinking at the bar, Neuwirth perused her notebook
of poetry and asked, "Did you ever think of writing songs?" Neuwirth
left their conversation by stating, "Next time I see you I want a song out
of you." Feeling inspired by this random event, Smith took his word and
began to write one.

Smith's early attempts at writing songs were at times awkward, as
she was experiencing the growing pains of turning her poetry into lyrics,
but Neuwirth continued to encourage her, seeing a talent in her that
she did not see at the time. Smith was able to expand her ideas by
putting them to music. To do so, she purchased a Martin acoustic guitar
on layaway from a pawnshop on 8th Avenue. Smith taught herself a few
chords from a Bob Dylan songbook, with her first song being "Fire of
Unknown Origin."

On June 5, 1970, Neuwirth took her to the Fillmore East to see
Crosby, Stills, Nash, and Young. Smith was especially taken by their
song "Ohio," which told the story of the Kent State riots, where four
unarmed college students were killed by the Ohio National Guard while
protesting the military operations that were happening in Cambodia at
the time. The incident drove a wedge between generations and increased the dissent that was evident among popular discourses. On the
positive side, Smith saw Young as more than just an entertainer but also
as a soundboard for societal responsibility and change.

The same night, Neuwirth introduced Smith to musician/producer
Todd Rundgren. After the concert, Neuwirth and Smith drove up to

Woodstock, New York, where Dylan's backing band, the Band, was recording its album *Stage Fright*, with Rundgren serving as the producer. Smith and Rundgren found that they had a lot in common and both had family from Upper Darby, Pennsylvania. The Rundgren association was not limited to just music. One night, Smith accompanied Rundgren to the Village Gate on Bleecker Street to see if there was any new talent that Rundgren could produce. Upon arriving, Smith and Rundgren saw the Holy Modal Rounders, a country/bluesy band that incorporated improvisational elements as well as psychedelic components. Smith could not keep her eyes off the drummer. Transfixed, Smith went backstage to meet him, who introduced himself as Slim Stewart.

The two struck a friendship where they would take walks during the evenings. One night, the two of them went to Max's Kansas City to get dinner. Jackie Curtis was there and immediately went to Smith and asked her, "What are you doing with Sam Shepard?" Smith unknowingly had struck a friendship with the famed playwright who at the time had won five Obie Awards and had a play being staged at Lincoln Center. By the time he was twenty-six, Shepard was already a prolific playwright, authoring close to twenty plays, including *La Turista* and *The Unseen Hand*. Smith was immediately smitten with Shepard, but he came with major baggage, including his wife O-Lan Johnson and a six-month-old son.

Smith continued to read her poetry to Mapplethorpe, who urged her to share her work with the public. Mapplethorpe made her promise to read her poems at a reading presented by the poet Jim Carroll. Smith continued to toil with her poetry, often finding that it was not physical enough, nor did it pack the punch of what she truly wanted to express. Mapplethorpe asked his friend Gerald Malanga if Smith could open for him at St. Mark's Church on February 10, 1971.

The event was put together by the Poetry Project, an organization dedicated to experimental poetry. Its programs featured a who's who of exciting poets, including Ginsberg, Frank O'Hara, and Ted Berrigan, to name a few. Excited by the prospect of reading at one of their events, Smith immediately started work to stand out and make a name for herself. Smith said, "My goal was not simply to do well, or hold my own. It was to make a mark at St. Mark's."

This moment proved to be the most important moment in her young professional life. First, she wanted to craft a more aggressive, in-your-face performance concept. Smith spoke of this design by declaring, "I wanted to infuse the written word with the immediacy and frontal attack of rock and roll." To help her with her idea, Shepard suggested that she put her words to music. Perusing her brain about whom she could utilize for the event, Smith remembered guitarist Lenny Kaye, a fixture on the scene at that time whom she would visit at his job at the record store Village Oldies on Bleecker Street. Being straightforward with him, Smith asked if he could "play a car crash with an electric guitar." Kaye accepted, and the two began to rehearse for the show.

The night of the show could not have been more kismet for the eager Smith. The evening drew an impressive crowd, including Mapplethorpe, Shepard, and Rundgren, as well as songwriter Lou Reed and artist Andy Warhol. Having Reed in the audience proved to be important for Smith, as the two would become musical compatriots. In Reed, Smith found a poetic colleague and likened him to noted New York poet Walt Whitman. While Smith found inspiration in jazz, which was a direct line to her improvisatory techniques, Reed provided her another way to improvise. Speaking to *Rolling Stone* in 2013, Smith stated, "One thing I got from Lou, that never went away, was the process of performing live over a beat, improvising poetry, how he moved over three chords for fourteen minutes. That was a revelation to me."

The evening proved to be extra special for Smith, as it was taking place on what would have been the seventy-fifth birthday of noted poet and playwright Bertolt Brecht, a most favorable sign for the evening. Poetry Project assistant director Anne Waldman introduced Smith, who was feeling a charge borne by the culmination of years of work along with the electricity of the room.

The reading served as an introduction of Patti Smith the performer. Dedicating the evening to "criminals from Cain to Genet," Smith began her reading with a poem entitled "Oath," with the opening line "Christ died for somebody's sins, but not mine." She continued with the poems "Fire of Unknown Origin," "The Devil Has a Hangnail," "Cry Me a River," and "Picture Hanging Blues." Smith ended her reading with "The Ballad of a Bad Boy," with Kaye implementing heavy chords and feedback. Feeling exhilarated, Smith left soon after with Sam, not saying good-bye, not apologizing for blowing their minds.

The affects of her reading were almost immediate. *Creem* magazine agreed to publish a suite of her poems. She was offered readings in

London and Philadelphia, a chapbook of poems for Middle Earth Books, and a possible record contract with Blue Sky Records. Feeling overwhelmed by the response that she received, Smith eschewed many of the offers, deciding instead to continuing working on her craft. The success of the reading perhaps spawned an overall creative flow to Smith that she had not experienced until then. One night while hanging out with Shepard, Smith and he collaborated on a play entitled *Cowboy Mouth*. The title was taken from the Dylan song "Sad Eyed Lady of the Lowlands," from the landmark album *Blonde on Blonde*. For the production, Shepard played the part of "Slim," a struggling artist trying to understand what art is and what it means to him. Smith played the part of "Cavale," a woman that eventually takes Slim hostage in an effort to make him famous.

Smith stated that the work wasn't so much a play but more akin to a "ritual" or a ceremony of sorts. The parts that Sam and Patti created for themselves involved a scene where the two characters have to spout improvised poetry at each other. Feeling hesitant, Smith did not know how to do this but was reassured by Shepard, who stated, "You can't make a mistake when you improvise." This one line set the stage for a skill that Smith would constantly fall back on throughout her professional career. The idea was that with creativity, she need not be afraid to try something new or fall on her face when doing so.

The resulting work appeared at the American Place Theater and was rife with insecurity and unevenness. The production was performed only once, as Shepard abruptly left the production before the second performance and made his way to New England without telling a soul. However, the experience solidified the desire for Smith to continue to perform, just not as an actress. Although her desire to perform was well formed at this time, it did not occur to her that she should use this hybrid mix as a means to front a rock-and-roll band. This was suggested to her by Sandy Pearlman, a renaissance man most known as the producer and manager for the rock band Blue Oyster Cult.

Smith mulled this suggestion over and decided to explore songwriting, aided by the few songs that she and Shepard performed in *Cowboy Mouth*. Through Shepard, Smith met Lee Crabtree, a songwriter and keyboardist whom Shepard performed with while a member of the Holy Modal Rounders. Crabtree was an eccentric fellow who also lived in the Chelsea. The two began a working relationship, but both were

initially too shy around each other. Crabtree eventually confided in
Smith that he was quite close to his grandfather, who left him a sizable
inheritance and his home. Crabtree's mom objected to the will and
tried to have him committed. Crabtree brought Smith to his grandfather's house, where he proceeded to break down and cry. This experience opened up their relationship such that they were free to explore
their musical tastes and ideas.

Following this incident, the two of them collaborated on "Dylan's
Dog," "Work Song," and further work on "Fire of Unknown Origin."
However, tragedy soon struck their brief friendship. Crabtree showed
up to her apartment one evening upset that his mother had blocked his
grandfather's will, resulting in his being denied his grandfather's house.
Smith gave him a T-shirt of a band that Sandy Pearlman was managing,
as it was raining heavily outside. After failing to show up for practice
one day, Smith asked around and found out that facing the loss of his
inheritance and possible institutionalization, Crabtree leapt to his death
from the roof of the Chelsea.

Stunned, Smith ventured forward with her writing. Pearlman introduced Smith to Allen Lanier, a keyboard player of the band he was
managing. First called Soft White Underbelly and then the Stalk-For-
rest Group, the band would eventually become the band Blue Oyster
Cult. Pearlman introduced the two of them, and they began a musical
and romantic relationship. Smith's creative juices began to churn in
many ways. Telegraph Books offered to publish an anthology of her
poems. Titled *Seventh Heaven*, the book included twenty-two poems
and off-putting black-and-white photography taken by Judy Linn.

On October 20, 1972, Smith decided to leave the apartment that she
had been sharing with Mapplethorpe. Smith soon moved in with Lanier
on East 10th Street, not too far away from the St. Mark's Church. On
New Year's Eve 1972, Smith went to the church for its annual marathon
reading. Combing through the poets that evening, Smith decided that a
career in regular poetry might not be the right fit for her. She knew that
1973 had to be her year—her year to strike out and become the artist
that she was meant to be. Although she understood that she was not
going to be a poet in the traditional sense, she knew that she was going
to get her brand of poetry heard one way or the other.

As it turned out, 1973 proved a promising year for Smith. Andy
Brown from Gotham Book Mart offered to publish a book of her

poems. With Allen paying their rent, Smith began to craft her second book of poems, which she entitled *Witt*. With this, Smith for the first time in her life was truly able to make a living as an artist. Although not entirely interested in acting again, Smith was asked by director Tony Ingrassia to star in a one-act play called *Identity*. Not wanting to continue her work at the Strand, Smith agreed to be in the play. The play was about a lesbian who has a dialogue with another girl. After not convincing the director that she could be a lesbian, Smith decided that this would be her last gig as an actor.

Smith wanted to continue the momentum, so she sought the professional advice of Jane Friedman, a PR executive who occasionally got Smith poetry-reading gigs at local bars. Many of those gigs were hostile, but Smith saw this as her paying her dues and a means of building her stage presence. Friedman booked Smith as an opening act for several bands, including the New York Dolls. Smith's act at this time was multidimensional to say the least. In addition to reading poetry, Smith fielded insults from the audience and sang songs accompanied by her cassette player. Most nights, Smith brought herself and the audience together by reciting a poem entitled "Piss Factory." The poem is about Smith's time working at a factory and how her moving to New York City represented her rebirth and renewal as a human being.

On Friday, July 13th, Smith gathered a reading at the loft of filmmaker Jack Smith. The reading was partly in tribute to Jim Morrison and was strongly attended. The success of the evening proved most intriguing to Friedman, who felt that Smith could be a new voice for a new generation. While Smith began to exercise her growing performance career, she began to contribute several pieces to notable periodicals of the era, including *Creem* and *Rock Scene*. Even with her journalistic endeavors, Smith carries herself as if she is amid one of her midsong improvisations. In an October 1974 piece for *Rock Scene* about the band Television, Smith eschews the normal journalistic etiquette of introducing the band members and instead begins the piece with a long tirade about image and the presentation of the "image." It's not until the fourth paragraph that Smith even lets on that this piece is about a band when she finally declares, "A group called TELEVISION who refuse to be a latent image but the machine itself!"

Similarly in a piece for *CREEM* entitled "jukebox cruci-fix," Smith rants about being at a party where she describes the scene as listening to the Doors' "Riders of the Storm" and then hearing the DJ interrupt the broadcast to announce that Morrison had passed away. The piece plays out like a half-realized nightmare but is an indication of how her poetic stylings were beginning to take shape and turn into stories. For example, a line in the piece states "Johnny Ace was cool he came east from Texas to knock 'just a dream' off the charts with 'pledging my love,'" which calls to mind a style that would make its way onto *Horses*, where it could have easily fit onto the album's titular song.

With their sights on performing, Smith and Kaye were at a loss as to where to bring their hybrid form of performance. Their style did not quite fit any particular mold, but the duo knew that what they had to offer the New York performance community was authentic and exciting. After their initial performance together, Smith and Kaye decided to expand their repertoire, which included more of Smith's poetry as well as covers such as "Speak Low," written by Kurt Weill, and "Annie Had a Baby," by Hank Ballard. On one occasion, Smith and Kaye performed at the West End Bar, a Beat poet establishment once frequented by Jack Kerouac and his literary compatriots. After the show, Jane gave them the great news that they were offered a six-day stint at Max's Kansas City, with their first show being on New Year's Eve. Their first performance saw the stars of the time in attendance: Ginsberg, Mapplethorpe, Shepard, and Rundgren, to name a few.

As a means of expanding the sonic qualities of their new group, Smith and Kaye decided to expand their instrumentation. They decided that a piano would be a good idea, seeing that the instrument possesses qualities both melodic and percussive. Smith and Kaye held an audition of sorts in a small room above the Victoria Theatre on 45th Street and Broadway. After several pianists were auditioned to unsatisfactory results, the last one to show up was Richard Sohl.

The nineteen-year-old Sohl possessed the qualities that Smith and Kaye were looking for in a pianist, having amassed a musical toolkit that could help them fulfill their musical vision. Soon after, the trio began to rehearse for their first gig at the West 13th Street hotspot Reno Sweeny's. Perhaps as a way of breaking him in, Kaye gave Sohl the nickname DNV because he thought that Sohl resembled Tadzio, the Polish boy from Luchino Visconti's *Death in Venice*. Slowly building their musical camaraderie, the trio decided to record their new sound to see if they could translate their live ferocity to tape.

With Kaye at the helm as producer and Mapplethorpe providing the funds, the trio recorded a single at Electric Lady Studios, founded by the late Jimi Hendrix. Smith had a short history with the studio but a history nonetheless, as she first visited the studio on its opening night while she was working as a journalist. Too shy to enter the party, Smith stood outside the steps of the studio and met Hendrix, who was leaving. Hendrix succumbed to drug-related asphyxia a mere month later.

Perhaps in tribute to Hendrix, the trio recorded his single "Hey Joe." Smith wanted to expand the melodic expression of what they were trying to capture by featuring another instrument. Smith invited Television guitarist Tom Verlaine to the session to satisfy the melodic requirements that she was looking for. Recording in Studio B, Smith, Kaye, and Sohl recorded the basic tracks. Afterward, Verlaine recorded two solo electric guitar tracks on top of the basic tracks.

Musically speaking, the song is an early example of Smith's use of adding to her original material to preexisting material. The opening features a spoken-word section where she deconstructs who Joe is by comparing Joe to Patty Hearst, the socialite and granddaughter of publishing luminary William Randolph Hearst. In 1974, Patty Hearst was kidnapped by, and later joined, the Symbionese Liberation Army, ultimately serving a two-year jail term for armed robbery. In Smith's rendition, Joe comes to represent the counterculture's disdain for corporate affluence, much in the way that the media spun Hearst's story. One could argue that in Hearst, Smith sees a spiritual sister or, at the very least, a fellow woman who refuses to settle for the patriarchal and corporate domination of their lives.

At the end of recording "Hey Joe," the group found itself with a few extra minutes of time. Smith and company decided to attempt a recording of "Piss Factory," with Kaye improvising over Sohl's performance and Smith riffing on the lyrics. What is most striking about the track and with the Smith/Kaye/Sohl permutation of the group is the sonic influence of jazz. Sohl vamps on a harmonic foundation that calls to mind pianist McCoy Tyner's performance on the seminal track "My Favorite Things," from John Coltrane's 1961 album of the same name, or pianist Red Garland's performance on the track "Milestones," from Miles Davis's 1958 album of the same name. All three songs are harmonically loose, particularly "Piss Factory," where Smith's lyrical execution sounds more like the bell of a saxophone than the sound of a human voice.

The mere instrumentation of the piece calls upon a political triumph in and of itself. With Sohl providing a clear harmonic background, Smith delivering a spoken-word fury, and Kaye providing an improvisational flair, the work proves to be the ultimate political dialogue, with Smith and Kaye representing two separate but powerful devices and Sohl setting the stage. Smith and Kaye's performances act like a musical debate, with Sohl moderating their exchanges.

While Smith would later employ her lyrics to metaphorically tell stories or heartfelt meanderings of the theme at hand, "Piss Factory" is explicit in its imagery of a blue-collar life without hopes and dreams. The narrative arc of the song is about free will—that no matter how grave the circumstances, we all have the right to live our lives as we see fit. In Smith's case, she would rather move to New York City and "never return, to burn out in this piss factory," with the "piss factory" in question being any situation where an individual may burn out and lose her hope.

With a physical representation of their sound ready to be heard, Kaye and Smith formed a record label entitled Mer and pressed fifteen hundred copies of their record at a small plant in Philadelphia. The record ultimately made its way to the jukebox at Max's Kansas City, where "Piss Factory," their improvised song, was played more often than their more fleshed-out rendition of "Hey Joe." Taking this as a positive sign, the group decided to continue to work on original material.

Finding new venues in which perform became a full-time gig for Smith. One evening, Smith and Kaye attended the New York premiere of the movie *Ladies and Gentleman, the Rolling Stones* at the Ziegfeld Theatre on West 54th Street. Afterward, Smith and Kaye ventured downtown to the Bowery to see the band Television perform at CBGB. Founded by Hilly Christal, the space was a dive bar to say the least but was open to most music. Standing for "country, bluegrass, blues," the only requirement that Kristal had was that the performers who graced the stage had to be new. In Kristal, Smith and company found a kindred spirit. Smith stated, "In NYC in the early '70s, there was no real place in NY for the new garde to experiment, but in 1973, Hilly Krystal opened the doors to CBGB so poets and musicians finally had a room of their own. Hilly was the good shepherd and William Burroughs was our guardian angel."

Not long after, the group began a several-week residency at Max's Kansas City, sharing the bill with Television. This stretch of time proved to be detrimental in the group's forming an eternal dialogue with one another. A few weeks later, the group performed at the Whiskey a Go Go in Los Angeles, at Rather Ripped Records in Berkeley, and at an audition night at the Fillmore West in San Francisco, with singer-songwriter Jonathan Richman accompanying the trio on drums. During the group's trip, it became clear to everyone that the band needed to expand its sound. The group decided that upon returning to New York, it would hold auditions for a second guitarist.

Placing an advertisement in the *Village Voice*, Smith and company auditioned several guitarists and settled on Czechoslovakian-born Ivan Kral. Smith enjoyed his raw style and stated, "He was energetic and open-minded, ready to magnify our swiftly developing concept of what rock and roll could be." Kral was already performing with several groups before joining the band, including CBGB scenesters Blondie. Kral was familiar with Smith's work, having already attended her poetry readings. With Kral joining the band, the group began to rehearse as well as perform at CBGB to further develop its sound.

The scene at CBGB slowly developed into a vital part of the New York City music community. The bands and performers at the club were of a wide variety and didn't exactly fit any particular mold. In addition to Smith and Television, groups such as the Ramones, with its simplistic two-minute anthems, and Blondie, with its synth-tinged tunes, began to perform. On one particular evening at CBGB, Arista Records president Clive Davis was in the crowd. In May of that year, Smith signed to Arista Records.

Davis's first encounter with Smith happened through a private showcase set up by Friedman. Along with Davis was A&R executive Bob Fieden, both of whom were interested in the group and the early buzz that it was receiving. The group performed a set of songs that left the two of them in chills. As Davis would later say, "when people ask me what are the most memorable performances I've ever seen, the ones that I'll never forget, definitely they would include Patti's." The relationship between Smith and Davis took the form of mutual admiration, with Davis having the utmost confidence in his newest signing. Davis later stated, "That was the core of our relationship: She presented her work; I gave her a frank assessment of which elements might prove to be bumps in the road."

On May 28, 1975, the group performed at a church on the Upper East Side to benefit local radio station WBAI. The group ended its set with a version of "Gloria," a hybrid song of sorts, merging Smith's poem "Oath" with the song "Gloria," written by Van Morrison for his band THEM. The band slowly began to build the song, where it reached new, exciting heights. By the end of the set, the group realized that all it was missing on its quest for rock-and-roll glory was a drummer. It found its drummer in Jay Dee Daugherty, a California transplant who ran the sound at CBGB.

The band's first performance with Daugherty was at the Bitter End, a club in Greenwich Village on Bleecker Street, right around the corner from where Patti lived at the time. The atmosphere was charged to say the least, with Davis being in the crowd and with the air of anticipation surrounding the band. On top of this, Bob Dylan was present, adding to the weight of the evening. However, history would prove that Smith had nothing to fear, as Davis was already impressed and smitten by Smith. In Smith, Davis saw an ambitious young woman who had the components needed to have a long-standing career in the music industry.

In April 1975, Smith was offered a seven-album recording contract with Arista for the tune of $750,000. What made the recording contract unique at the time was that Smith demanded complete creative control of her material—a rarity, especially among new artists such as Patti. Furthermore, Smith had final say over advertising campaigns and authority over the production of her albums. Arista's signing the group was a clear indication that Smith was on the verge of something new, and it shined a bright spotlight on the CBGB community.

A shift within the expectations of female-fronted groups was about to happen . . . with Patti at the helm.

3

"WITH LOVE WE SLEEP"

1974–1975

By the mid-1970s, it became apparent how much of a business the music industry had become. The disparity between the artist and the audience became more prevalent, and the marketing of the performer began to outweigh the artistic merit of the music. Nothing was more indicative of the marketing scheme of American artists than the album covers that adorned the shelves of record stores. In the year that Smith's debut album *Horses* was released, album covers released by female artists showcased a variety of sexual tropes, standards, and concepts of beauty.

Singer-songwriter Anne Murray's album *Together* features a close-up of her face, with most of her dirty blonde locks out of the frame—the focal point of the picture being Murray's piercing blue eyes and ever so slightly creased mouth, perhaps indicating desire. On the other side of the spectrum, disco superstar Donna Summer's album *Love to Love You Baby* shows the singer from her midsection, with her hands toward the middle of her body, suggesting that she is pleasuring herself. This idea is enhanced with her head tilting back and her mouth open, suggesting a heightened sense of pleasure or arousal. Singer-songwriter Carly Simon's album *Playing Possum* shows the artist's profile from the nose down while she is wearing black lingerie and knee-high black boots. The lack of seeing her face in its entirety warrants the conclusion that Simon is merely a sexual object, not an artist.

However sexual or oversexual these examples seem in the greater historical context of female artistry, the cover of Smith's *Horses* would prove to resemble a symbol of defiance and sexual liberation, simultaneously breaking the rules and redefining the sexual boundaries for female musicians for the rest of time.

Shot by Mapplethorpe in the apartment of Sam Wagstaff, the album features Smith leaning against a wall, wearing black trousers and a white button-up shirt, with a jacket thrown over her shoulder in a very Sinatra-esque fashion. While reminiscent of a Rat Pack outlier, Smith's look could also be seen as a direct throwback to the French poets who inspired her. In one fell swoop, Mapplethorpe captured the artistic integrity of Smith while selling the world the female embodiment of punk rock.

However classic the album cover has become or how calculated the meaning of the picture was assembled at the time that it was shot, Arista Records was none too pleased with the result. Clive Davis's initial response was unfavorable and perhaps with good reason, as he had a new artist that he had to sell to the marketplace, which may be confused with her image. Davis later stated, "I admit, at first I was conflicted about the image; I was aware of its power, but with my label-president concern, I thought it might confuse the uninitiated." Furthermore, Arista wanted to airbrush the slight mustache that Smith had above her lip. Smith vetoed the suggestion, stating, "I felt it would be like having plastic surgery or something." Although Davis had his reservations, his complete trust in Smith and her artistic presence won him over, and he allowed the picture to be on the cover.

The androgynous undercurrent is not so much the question at hand but what the picture evokes to the person looking at it. Smith was privy to the occasional comment regarding her supposed "androgynous" style. One night at Max's Kansas City, someone asked if she was androgynous "like Mick Jagger." Smith in her characteristically cool demeanor took this as a compliment, feeling that the comment meant a dual characteristic or, as she said, "both beautiful and ugly at the same time."

Whether one thinks of her as a man or as a woman, there is an undeniable beauty to her that may make one either comfortable or uncomfortable. Feminist theorist Camille Paglia in her book *Sex, Art, and American Culture* notes that while the cover depicts "one of the greatest pictures of a woman," she likened Smith to a "half-transvestite" and an "anorexic Frank Sinatra." Art critic Paul Taylor knew nothing of Smith's work but bought the album *because* of the cover, ultimately proving Davis's initial hesitation to be untrue. Taylor stated, "I bought the album based on the strength of the photograph. It was elegant and totally modern."

As iconic as the cover of *Horses* has become, neither Smith nor Mapplethorpe consciously set out to make rock-and-roll history with the picture. What is known is that Mapplethorpe did have certain intentions with the photograph. For starters, he wanted to use natural light, which adds to the natural softness and definition to the picture. Upon the thirtieth anniversary of the album's release, Smith told *New York Magazine* that constructing the shot was more flippant than one might think. Mapplethorpe took twelve photos in total, with the eighth being the winner and Mapplethorpe alerting Smith that they got the shot. Smith replied, "How do you know? And he said, 'I just know,' and I said, 'Okay. And that was it."

The title of the album itself warrants discussion, as a horse has many cross-cultural attributes. In Freudian analysis, the horse is a symbol of sexual expression, which can be both negative and positive depending on what the result is. In context with Smith's album, the horse serves as the umbrella term for the songs that it houses; the horse can be seen as liberation of sorts. Furthermore, the idea of the horse can be seen as a symbol of femininity. Evidence of this comes directly from Smith herself, who at the suggestion of Mapplethorpe wrote an elegy for socialite Edie Sedgwick upon her death. Smith stated that to fulfill this elegy, she was "obliged to consider what it meant to be female, I entered the core of my being, led by the girl poised before a white horse." An additional meaning could be that the horse represents a sort of prize or acquisition. Smith stated that when thinking about the people with whom she came up through the Chelsea ranks, many of them did not make it, or they succumbed to circumstances. But in Mapplethorpe and about her early years in New York City, she felt, "It was I who got one of the best horses." One could assume that the idea of the horse was something that was one of a kind, something that was Smith's and Smith's alone.

In the early summer of 1975, Smith and the group began to rehearse in preparation for their debut album. The group began to record the album on September 2, 1975, at Electric Lady Studios. The studio itself was a large basement space, which had been a country-and-western club for thirty years and briefly a rock venue called Generation Club before Jimi Hendrix bought the building in 1968, intending to operate the space as his own club. Instead, his engineer, Eddie Kramer, convinced him to turn it into a recording studio.

Smith and Kaye decided on John Cale, a member of the Velvet Underground as well as a producer on albums by Nico and Iggy Pop as the producer for the record. The Welsh musician/producer was born in Garnant, Wales, in 1942 and studied music at the University of London, where his compositional motives leaned toward the avant-garde. Upon arriving in New York, Cale began to perform with several luminaries of the avant-garde scene at the time, including John Cage and LaMonte Young. Alongside Lou Reed, Cale cofounded the Velvet Underground in 1965 but eventually left in 1968 over creative differences with Reed.

Smith's decision to pick Cale would, ironically, provide foreshadowing as to how many people would discover Smith. Smith picked Cale after seeing the cover to his 1974 album *Fear* and commenting, "Now there's a set of cheekbones." The sessions proved to be fruitful, if not difficult at times, as Smith and Cale occasionally butted heads over creative differences. When asked what it was like working with Cale, Smith later stated, "It's like 'A Season in Hell'. He's a fighter and I'm a fighter so we're fightin'. Sometimes fightin' produces a champ."

While the group was more concerned with having a great-sounding record, Cale had a bigger picture in mind for the songs, which included adding auxiliary instruments, such as a string orchestra. Although the group eschewed such suggestions, what Cale did do for the group is finally turn it into a cohesive unit. Cale helped the musicians innately absorb their sound, which then allowed them to step outside the music that they had been accustomed to performing.

Before Cale confronted the band about the songs themselves, his initial step in the process was to find the right sounds from the instruments that the band members had at their disposal. Being the strict disciplinarian, Cale tuned each instrument himself; however, he was not satisfied with the way that the group sounded. Cale then gave the band members all new instruments, much to their chagrin. He then set his sights on working on the band's material, fleshing out ideas and honing in on the more abstract tracks on the record.

Although the sessions resulted in a landmark album, Smith was dissatisfied with Cale as a producer as she wanted a producer who would have been more of a technician then Cale's made genius persona. Smith later stated, "I had to solidify everything I believed. We came into the studio half-assed and glib, then I had to pound my fists into his skull day and night."

One of the major themes on *Horses* is religion, the challenging of it as an institution, the role of it in one's life, and so forth. The album's opening track, "Gloria," is a prime example of how Smith challenges the role of religion. "Gloria" is less of an introduction to Smith's musical prowess and more a manifesto of what was to come. Originally written by Van Morrison for his group THEM, the original lyrics speaks of a sexual conquest. Smith maintains the pronoun "she," which does not change the gender roles of the song but perhaps puts her in Morrison's story as the sexual conquest. Smith's playfulness with the song calls on the identity of whoever is singing the song. "Gloria" speaks of a sexual escapade, which causes Smith, as a woman, to cover a different identity position and, in the process, a reversal of sexual intent. The song is not a cover so to speak but rather a reworking of the song's intent and scope. The result is more of a pastiche than a cover per se.

The song's opening line, "Jesus died for somebody's sins but not mine," is Smith's rejection of the idea that her transgressions somehow caused the demise of Jesus Christ. Furthermore, with this declaration, Smith is absolving herself of her wrongdoings and giving herself a clean slate. However, Smith is a religiously devoted woman and a woman of faith. Smith later said, "The statement of that song was a declaration of existence; it was not against Jesus Christ."

One mustn't forget how powerful an opening line this is, especially when you look back at what some of the popular music 1975 had to offer—from the gentle country crooning of Glen Campbell's "Rhinestone Cowboy" to the easy listening of Captain and Tennille's "Love Will Keep Us Together" to the bravado of top-40 rock provided by Aerosmith. Popular radio at this time was not churning out anthems about religious contravention and sexual conquests . . . especially from a debut album by a woman.

The next three lines speak of the assimilation of religious themes, the strengthening of one's heart, and the ultimate acceptance of one's past. The music ultimately reflects the themes that Smith aims to deliver, changing dynamics to reflect the intent and emotion of the lyrics. The soft bass and piano introduction reflects an organlike timbre that easily points to the song's religious preface. What makes the song most exciting is the group's utilization of tempo shifts and articulation to carry the listener to its ultimate fervor. Relying on the simple punk chord progression of E major, D major, and A major, the group slowly crescendos to the song's climax while increasing the dynamics of the music.

In direct opposition to the stunning "Gloria" is the album's second track, "Redondo Beach," a blues-inspired reggae track that Smith wrote the lyrics to in 1971. Smith wrote the lyrics while her sister Linda was staying with Mapplethorpe and her at the Chelsea. After an argument, Linda stormed out of the apartment into the New York City ether. Nearing nightfall, Smith was concerned, as she did not return. As a means of trying to clear her head, Smith took the F train all the way south to Coney Island. Sitting on the beach, Smith sat with her thoughts as the sun rose. Upon coming home, she wrote a first draft of the lyrics. As she woke, she saw that Linda had made it home, safe and sound.

"Redondo Beach" follows a clearly definable blues progression of I-IV-V. For this particular song, Cale asked for Smith to dial back the faux-Jamaican tone that she had adopted for a more reserved, laid-back sound that was equally evocative of the song's tone. The song's tone masks the truly horrible theme behind the lyrics, which tells the story of a "pretty little girl" who "was the victim of sweet suicide." Juxtaposed with the song's upbeat reggae beat and style, the result perfectly matches the emotional duality that such an exercise can offer.

The jazz influences that began to show their head with "Piss Factory" made their way onto the album's third track, "Birdland." Smith was inspired to write the lyrics to this song after reading *A Book of Dreams*, by Peter Reich. The book tells the story of the relationship between the author and his father, philosopher Wihelm Reich. The lyrics interpret the author's feelings of loss upon the death of his father. At the funeral, the boy imagines that the limousines stationed at the cemetery become UFOs and take him away from the funeral. Smith and Co. clearly try to mimic that hallucinatory illusion by creating a whirlwind of sonic fury. Kaye incorporates feedback and drones that peak and crash against Sohl's straight-ahead playing.

Lasting a total of 9 minutes 15 seconds, "Birdland" clearly takes the spirit of an improvisational piece as opposed to a rock-and-roll song. With this song, one gets a sense of what Smith's early poetry readings were like, which included improvisational aspects. Furthermore, the influence of late-era John Coltrane can be felt throughout the track, as Coltrane in his later years was sonically searching for a divine purpose, which Smith and Co. are equally searching for via the thoughts that the young Peter Reich may have been feeling at his father's funeral.

From the initial offering that the first three songs from *Horses* provide, Smith and Co. were showcasing more of the ethos of punk rock as opposed to a particular style or popularization thereof. While punk rock dictates the musical "middle finger" to the status quo, it's ultimately the image of punk rock that stirred the status quo. Whether it was the leather-clad stoicism that the Ramones demonstrated or the bratty, safety-pinned couture that the Sex Pistols advertised, Smith promoted the punk rock ideology by trying to show a varied musical appetite. From the rock-driven "Gloria" to the reggae-tinged "Redondo Beach" to the jazz-inflected "Birdland," Smith was providing the popular music community with a clear definition of what punk is.

Completing the first side of the album is "Free Money," a fairly straight-ahead rock song about winning the lottery and being able to afford luxuries for a better life. The song begins with a beautiful introduction by Sohl, gentle and lyrical before the drums enter. The tempo of the song slowly crescendos as the rest of the group enters on the verse. The use of the sudden shifts in tempo is the storytelling device of the piece, mirroring the emotional whirlwind of going from having no money to having it all.

Throughout the song, Smith speaks of going to sleep where she sees "those dollar bills go swirling 'round my bed." Smith compares dreaming to a form of currency, which she does often and henceforth is "rich"—perhaps a subtle indication to herself that future riches, both conscious and unconscious, were obtainable.

The second side of the album begins with the song "Kimberly," an ode to Smith's little sister and the tale of an instance where Smith was holding her outside during a lightning storm while she was a baby. An antithesis to the way that the shift in tempos helped shape the narrative of "Free Money," the destructive lightning storm of "Kimberly" is not the focal point of the song but rather Smith's confidence that the storm would subside, paired with the easygoing, breezy feel of the song. Beginning with a gentle swell on the organ from Sohl, the repetitive nature of the bass playing B, E, F# suggests a firm, confident harmonic palate. Smith speaks of the storm being an otherworldly event, or perhaps the line "the fates calling you" alludes to the idea that mother nature had something important in store for Kimberly. In conjunction with this notion, Smith allegorizes herself as a modern-day Joan of Arc with the lyric "And I feel like just some misplaced Joan of Arc," suggesting that she is on a crusade of some sort.

The subsequent track "Break It Up" is most indicative of 1970s, bravado-laden lead guitar sound that came to saturate the decade. This is largely due to the contribution of Tom Verlaine, who contributed the lead guitar track and received a cowriter credit of the song. Lyrically, "Break It Up" speaks about escapism and shedding one's mortal coil. Smith speaks about seeing "the boy break out of his skin," alluding to a person/presence leaving one's body and journeying into the afterlife. In a December 1975 interview with *Crawdaddy* magazine, Smith stated that the "boy" in question was Jim Morrison. She had a dream where she went into a clearing and saw Morrison in human form lying in a marble slab. Though human, his wings were made of stone and were not allowing him to be free. In an effort to set him free, Smith shouted at him "Break It Up! Break It Up!" until his wings finally broke through and he was able to be free.

Horses ends with the track "Land," which is broken into three excerpts: "Horses," "Land of a Thousand Dances," and "La Mer(de)." The trilogy of songs that ends *Horses* exhibits Smith as a storyteller/narrator, as the song plays out as a strange after-school special or a twisted public service announcement.

"Horses" tells the story of Johnny, who at the onset of the song is drinking a glass of tea in a hallway. From the location, we can assume that Johnny is an adolescent and in a school. Further into the introduction of the song, Johnny sees another boy, who confronts Johnny and presses him against a locker where "he drove it home he drove it deep in Johnny." The phrase "drove" implies that Johnny is the victim of rape, and the after-mentioned "Johnny fell on his knees" suggests that an assault took place. Now, the identity of Johnny is open to interpretation. The most obvious is that Johnny is in fact Mapplethorpe, who for a while earned money as a gay hustler and would be privy to such sexual circumstances and the danger that comes from them.

Another interpretation of the Johnny character is that he is the physical embodiment of rock and roll. During the midseventies, the music business became an all-encompassing figurehead that presided over the popular culture. By this time in American popular music, big-business bands, such as Grand Funk Railroad, Steely Dan, and the Allman Brothers, and light saccharine pop, such as Tony Orlando and Dawn, were slowly permeating the reaction that the late-1960s counterculture was fighting against. This left a void for aggressive, spirited rock music that had not only a message but the panache behind it, effectively violating the spirit of rock and roll to some extent.

One could see the sexual assault that Johnny encounters in the hallway as the music business raping the very soul of rock and roll by clouding his thoughts with so-called horses, which in this context can represent any evil or negative figure. Smith contextualizes Johnny's poignant demise as mirrored in the horses themselves and the "white shining silver studs with their nose in flames." Additionally, the leather jacket that Johnny sports can represent the youth culture of the time, and the obvious cocaine allegory of the "snow" that went up his nose can be viewed as the excess that was rapidly deteriorating the spirit of rock and roll and clouding its collective memory.

The album's closing track is the song "Elegie," which Smith wrote in tribute to Jimi Hendrix. To commemorate the fifth anniversary of his passing, Smith insisted that the song be recorded on the very day itself: September 18, 1975. Cowritten and featuring Allan Lanier, the song is less of an elegy by definition and more of a haunting ballad or requiem for those that have past. Beginning with the piano and bass playing off each other with a heavily reverberated guitar resonating throughout, Smith begins by playing against the atmosphere upon reciting "I just don't know what to do tonight," evoking a sense of restlessness. Smith ends the song by stating, "I think it's sad, it's much too bad our friends can't be with us today," ending the album in dedication to those she has loved and those she has lost.

The album was met with near universal acclaim by the popular press and critics alike. Those in favor of the album were quick to realize the multidimensional themes it contained. John Rockwell, in his review in *Rolling Stone*, stated that "the range of concerns in *Horses* is huge, far beyond what most rock records even dream of," perhaps alluding to the music of the time. Furthermore, Rockwell contextualizes the importance of the album by stating, "To say that any of these songs is 'about' anything in particular is silly—it limits them in a way that hopelessly confines their evocativeness. Like all real ports, Smith offers visions that embrace a multiplicity of meanings, all of them valid if they touch an emotional chord."

Other critics were polarized by the album's mix of philosophical elements with rock and roll. In his review, critic Robert Christgau mentions her then new voice while calling out her use of postmodern themes. Christgau stated, "I don't feel much intelligent sympathy for Smith's apocalyptic romanticism. Her ideas are as irrelevant to any social apocalypse I can envision as they are to my present as a well-adjusted, well-rewarded media professional." In their review, *Creem* magazine likened *Horses* to those outside the punk/modern discourse. They stated, "With her wealth of promise and the most incandescent flights of and stillnesses of this album she joins the ranks of people like Miles Davis, Charlie Mingus, or the Dylan of 'Sad Eyed Lady' and Royal Albert Hall."

Perhaps on a stranger note, the British music press was mixed in their response to the record. Famed *Melody Maker* stated that the album was "precisely what's wrong with rock and roll right now." On the other side of the coin, the British music paper *Sounds* stated, "Ladies and gentlemen, I give you the record of the year. Quite simply this is one of the most stunning, commanding, engrossing platters to come down the turnpike since John Lennon's *Plastic Ono Band*, and for the same reasons."

To this day, *Horses* continues to ride the legacy of a classic record of a modern genre. In 2009, *Rolling Stone* compiled its list of the "500 Greatest Albums of All Time," with *Horses* reaching the plump spot of number 44, sandwiched between the Band's *The Band* and Pink Floyd's *Dark Side of the Moon*. Singer Michael Stipe of REM noted that *Horses* was the reason that he decided to become a musician. Stipe stated, "[The album] tore my limbs off and put them back on in a whole different order. I was like 'Shit, yeah, oh my god!' then I threw up."

However, not everyone shares in the album's legacy. On July 20, 2005, the blog *Flaming Pablum* published the article "In Damnation of . . . *Horses* by Patti Smith." In the article, the author stated,

"Drenched in self-indulgent melodrama, however, Horses sounds more at home rubbing shoulders with the hoary likes of Meat Loaf than with comparatively spartan albums recorded by Smith's fellow CBGB's alumni like the Ramones and the Dead Boys." The "melodrama" of which the author speaks indicates the poetic style that Smith made her own with *Horses*, which nearly thirty years later continues to challenge modern-day thoughts.

Before and after the release of *Horses*, Arista began to market Smith to numerous periodicals. The band's first New York appearance after the release of *Horses* was a three-night, seven-show stint at the Bottom Line from December 26 to December 28. The first show was hyped as a make-or-break moment for Smith; it was an Arista showcase for the national and international press in her hometown. A lot was riding on it. A *New York Times* article touted her, along with Joel Zoss and Tom Waits, under the heavy title "They Speak for Their Generation."

The show establishes the different personas that Smith inhabits based on what she is performing. During this time, it was not uncommon for Smith to be her own opening act. She would often come out first and do a spoken word–poetry hybrid, with Kaye accompanying her. Afterward, the band would join them onstage and begin their set.

In his *New York Times* review, critic John Rockwell examines both personalities that she showcased. Describing the spoken-word portion, he described Smith as "scared or stoned": "the phrases were jerky and fragmentary" and "wavered off into girlish ramblings, punctuated by giggles and pockmarked by memory lapses." However, he later described Smith and the band's performance as "terrifying in its intensity, like some cosmic, moral struggle between demons and angels." Rockwell's description paints the picture that Smith was gaining more confidence with the band and slowly moving away from the previous paradigm of spoken word followed by music.

The beginning of 1976 saw the music business machine placing Patti and the band in full promotional swing. This meant more touring and developing regional interest while Arista worked to promote the record. From January 1 to 4, the group performed a short residency at My Father's Place, the Long Island equivalent of CBGB, before heading on the road for engagements in Boston, Washington, DC, Atlanta, Cleveland, and San Francisco. The following month, Smith and the group performed a string of shows on the West Coast at a breakneck pace, with four shows over at the Aztec Center at San Diego State University (February 3–4), four shows at the Golden Bear in Huntington Beach (February 6–8), and ten shows thereafter (February 11–15).

Within this maze of media attention, concert dates, and tireless promotion came the most profound moment of her life. On March 9, 1976, Smith was introduced to guitarist Fred "Sonic" Smith of the Detroit-based rock band the MC5. Kaye introduced the pair at a party thrown by Arista records in Detroit at the twenty-four-hour hot dog establishment American Coney Island.

Frederick Dewey Smith was born on September 14, 1949, in West Virginia but soon moved to Detroit. At the age of twelve, Smith began to play guitar and performed with a number of local bands before joining the MC5 in the mid-1960s. Alongside vocalist Rob Tyner, guitarist Wayne Kramer, bassist Michael Davis, and drummer Dennis Thompson, the bandmates were the forefathers of the "Detroit Sound," a low-fidelity, high-energy, politically charged music that was a precursor to punk rock. By 1968, the group had become Detroit's most buzz-worthy band, with a performance at the disaster that was the 1968 Democratic National Convention, which secured the musicians a recording contract with Elektra Records. Their 1969 record *Kick Out the Jams*, with the album's title track beginning with the rallying cry "Kick out the jams motherfuckers!" cemented their place in the 1960s counterculture movement and placed them in direct opposition with the stereotyped flower-power hippie vibe of then modern America.

At the time of their meeting, Fred was twenty-seven years old and led a group called the Sonic Rendezvous Band, which was up and coming following the dissolution of the MC5. That night, Patti invited him onstage with the band to perform their encore rendition of the Who's "My Generation." They spent that night together and promised each other that they would stay in touch, starting an intense, albeit difficult, long-distance relationship on the telephone.

That same month, Patti and the group performed a series of shows on the East Coast with tour dates in New York, Westport (Connecticut), and Washington, DC. With the added media attention came more opportunities for Smith to market the record via television. On April 17, 1976, Smith and the group performed "Gloria" on *Saturday Night Live*. The performance showcases Smith as a confident force to be reckoned with, as she struts and sways with the tempo. With Smith sporting similar clothing to that she donned on the cover of *Horses*, one must think that this was a calculated execution of bridging the visual aspect of Smith's performance. Along with her ease onstage, Smith puts her hands on her hips with a sense of fearlessness that is met with cheers from the audience. In conclusion to the performance, Smith signs off by saying "Happy Easter CBGB."

Less than a month later, on May 11, 1976, Smith appeared on the BBC show *The Old Grey Whistle Test*, which was one of the most popular and heavily watched shows in England. For such an important program, the group could have performed material that was polished and that it could perform at the drop of a hat. At this time, any of its repertory from *Horses* would have sufficed. For its British television debut, the group decided to perform "Horses" and "Hey Joe."

Playing "Hey Joe" was a big risk for the band, which was not that familiar with the song. Smith stated, "We were walking a tightrope, playing an arrangement of a song we'd never played. Lenny and Richard knew what it was and where to go, JD and I concentrated on playing the proper notes." In comparison with her performance on *Saturday Night Live*, Smith appears to take a more calculated approach to her performance. She begins the performance wearing sunglasses, which she dramatically throws off her face shortly after beginning. She performs as a character, a headstrong rock-'n'-roll star waving her musical hand to the British music press.

After completing "Horses," the group effortlessly segues into "Hey Joe," where Smith improvises different scraps and string bends on her guitar, perhaps in an effort to evoke the spirit of Hendrix. Smith may have also been trying to curry favor with the British media by her performance of the song, as Hendrix was initially heralded by the British press before being accepted in America. One must think that Smith might be trying to mirror such a marketing scheme. Whether conscious or not, the performance is striking and introduces a more adventurous Smith to the British press. The tactic worked. Following several shows, the group returned to England to perform at the Roundhouse for two shows on May 15 and 16. Before its appearance on *The Old Grey Whistle Test*, ticket sales for the shows were slow but had since increased severalfold.

Interest in the band continued to expand, and the machine demanded more. Without missing a beat, the band seamlessly went back to the studio to record the follow-up to *Horses*: a record it titled *Radio Ethiopia*.

4

"TILL VICTORY"

1975–1978

Corruption and a lack of trust in our political figures reigned heavily over the consciousness of America. On August 9, 1974, Richard Nixon resigned as the president of the United States amid the Watergate scandal and the resulting fallout. In January 1976, Jimmy Carter, the fresh-faced governor of Georgia, won the Democratic primary, where he would go up against incumbent Gerald Ford, whose presidency was soiled by what some thought was the unconscionable task of pardoning Nixon for his crimes.

America was disgusted. America was fragile. Patti Smith was on fire.

Concurrent to the national politics that were permeating, several of Patti's compatriots from CBGB were in the process or had already released their first albums, showcasing the diversity of the New York City punk rock scene. In April 1976, the Ramones released their self-titled debut album on Sire Records, which opened with "Blitzkrieg Bop," one of the group's most recognized and revered songs. Subsequent debut records from Blondie, Television, and Talking Heads demonstrated the wealth of talent the scene had to offer, with Television's "Marquee Moon" sounding less like a stereotypical punk record and more an avant-garde amalgamation of jazz and rock. The Talking Heads' album *Talking Heads: 77* spawned the minor hit "Psycho Killer," which married art school aesthetic with a clearly defined hook and chorus. Now Smith and Co. had the unenviable task of following up the juggernaut that was *Horses*. Eyes and ears were firmly planted on Patti in a way that she never saw before.

Her follow-up record, *Radio Ethiopia*, was credited to the Patti Smith Group, creating a broader ensemble record, as opposed to *Horses*, which was billed simply under "Patti Smith." Furthermore, whereas *Horses* employed a broad harmonic palette, *Radio Ethiopia* was a play on extremes with the hard-rock bravado of "Ask the Angels" and "Pumping (My Heart)" to the lethargic, stoned-out rock of "Ain't It Strange" and "Poppies" to the album's ten-minute free-rock opus "Radio Ethiopia/Abyssinia."

Smith was initially interested in an overall better-sounding record when the group began preliminary sessions for *Radio Ethiopia*. Smith told a reporter in *Hit Parader*, "I wanted this record to sound reasonably good over the radio." To help Smith with her plan, producer Jack Douglas was enlisted to help Patti reach her goal. Douglas at that time was well known for his contributions to several Aerosmith records, including *Get Your Wings*, *Toys in the Attic*, *Rocks*, and *Draw the Line*, and would ultimately produce the legendary John Lennon album *Double Fantasy*. Additionally, Smith's representation felt that he was up to the task, having produced more spoken word–heavy albums by Allen Ginsberg with Bob Dylan and Yoko Ono.

From the beginning, Smith and Douglas wanted to make a work of art, something that could be artistically fulfilling as well as a contemporary statement on rock music. Douglas stated, "This is one of Patti's favorites. The idea was, 'what's the limit? How far can we go?' We wanted to make a piece of art, even though Clive Davis was saying, 'Where's the single?' But we didn't want to fall into that kind of thinking."

Continuing with the introduction/body/conclusion format that *Horses* established, the opening track to *Radio Ethiopia* begins with the song "Ask the Angels," a rallying call to end the virus of complacency and move forward toward revolution and rebellion. From the opening salvo of "Move!" Smith pushes the listeners to feel beyond their scabbed-over psyches and instead reach within themselves to fuel the fire of their desire. Smith parses how far-reaching this sense of complacency is by stating that she has seen it "across the country through the fields." The production of the song echoes this sentiment, with the "wall of guitar" sound reflecting the brevity of Smith's lyrics.

"Ask the Angels" clearly shows the intent to get the band on the radio, as it aimed for the masses, as opposed to any old audience at CBGB. Gone was the lo-fi aesthetic that Cale brought to the table with *Horses*, and coming to light was the pop precision that Douglas proved confident with. The song feels oddly out of place on the record: a stiff upper lip–style homage to the spirit of rock and roll, followed by a fairly mellow-sounding group of songs. After the power-pop, top-40 precision of "Ask the Angels," Smith follows up with the heroin-themed song "Ain't It Strange." The imagery of the song delves deep into the murky unconscious of one who is under the influence of heroin. The guitar mirrors such ideas with upbeats that are slightly behind the rest of the band, invoking the sense that a junkie is nodding off and lacking coherence.

With "Ain't It Strange," Smith juggles with what God is and the complicated role of God in one's life. Smith decries, "Come and join me, I implore thee," daring and taunting God to make his move. Smith later on asks, "True true, who are you?" followed by "Who who am I?" This statement breaks the wall down between Smith and God, which the band mirrors by dramatically changing keys and expanding its dynamics from soft to loud. This direct and audacious plea from Smith to God to speak to her cements her identity as someone who acknowledges God but also wants to be part of the religious discourse that such an acknowledgment would bring.

This quasi-coherent line between consciousness and unconsciousness and the otherworldly that "Ain't It Strange" displays segues brilliantly into the subsequent track, "Poppies." In the literal sense of the word, "poppy" could refer to the narcotic use of the plant of the same name, which is found in drug circles via opium. Symbolically, the word "poppy" has been used as an indicator for sleep and death, the latter indicator due to its striking red color. Additionally, the idea of the poppy being a symbol of sleep plays out in *The Wonderful Wizard of Oz*, by L. Frank Baum, in which the main characters of the story are threatened by a magical poppy field, which scares them into thinking that they will sleep forever.

The lyrical content of "Poppies" calls on the Beat style of prose, or what Ginsberg called "the spontaneous mind": a free-associative, stream-of-consciousness kind of style. The way that Patti embellishes her lyrics calls on the vocal embellishments that Jim Morrison would incorporate, which is further heightened by Sohl's vibrato-infused electric piano playing, which calls on the performing style of the Doors' keyboardist Ray Manzarek. The influence of Morrison on the song is supported by the liner notes of *Radio Ethiopia,* where Smith dictates that the song was inspired by Morrison, Andy Warhol socialite Edie Sedgwick, and the Queen of Sheba.

In Sedgwick, Smith found a heroine, or the image of what she imagined heroism to be. Speaking to Penny Green for *Interview* in 1973, Smith details that alongside Rimbaud, Sedgwick, and Brian Jones, she always worshipped the "hero-god" because she herself could not speak directly with God. Smith states, "The closest, most accessible god was a hero-god: Brian Jones, Edie Sedgwick, or Rimbaud because their works were there, their voices were there, their faces were there. I was very image-oriented."

"Poppies" displays one of the most complex examples of Smith's juxtaposition of poetry and rock and roll. To aid in this display is Douglas's expertly executed use of background voices to help propel the narrative. The main allegory of the song tells the tale of an individual looking to score drugs and her ultimate descent into an overdose. The protagonist of this allegory is most likely Sedgwick, who died of an overdose at the all-too-young age of 28 in 1971. Douglas uses several tracks of Smith's voice as a call and response with her own voice. Smith sings about the character experiencing the effects of the drugs as she descends "through the dorsal spine and down and around," while a separate track hauntingly responds with "I want more." This effect conjures the idea that the third person could very well be Smith and that the first-person response is Smith looking back in the first person of her experiences.

Douglas's use of backing vocals as a call-and-response device is evident on the album's first single, "Pissing in a River." A basic reading of the lyrical content would result in an understanding that Smith is longing for the romantic approval of a suitor. Smith pours her heart out to her suitor and asks him, "What more can I give you to make this thing grow?" Smith asked the suitor to "Come come come," with the rest of the band acting as her Greek chorus by responding with "Take me back!"

However, the religious undertones of the song are equally valid to the aforementioned lover's discourse. First, the use of the word "river" denotes the transfer of water, itself a symbol of fertility, life, and re-birth. For Smith to state that she's "pissing in a river" could mean that she sullied life with some sort of filth: that the introduction of bodily waste into a pure element negates the positive attributes of the "river."

Furthermore, when Smith says, "Should I pursue a path so twisted, should I crawl defeated and gifted," she is exclaiming, "Should I leave this supposed life of sin and move toward a life?" although "twisted" is in fact a worthy and "gifted" life. Smith ultimately chooses the life toward a life that is "twisted" but "pissing in the river." Harmonically, the song maintains a stable chord progression of A minor, C major, D minor, F major, giving Kaye a stable harmonic component to improvise freely when needed or mirror the emotional capacity of Smith's lyrics.

The album's second single, "Pumping (My Heart)," is a prime exam-ple of the more finessed production style that Douglas was able to provide the record. Beginning with Sohl actively striking Db octaves on the piano and giving the song an overall powerful and energetic feel, the band perfectly executes the raucous three-minute hit single check-list: powerful vocals, crunchy guitars, and sing-a-long choruses.

Lyrically, Smith makes an ode to boxing and uses the act of boxing as a metaphor for love or any fight that is worth fighting. By stating, "Baby gotta box in the center of the ring and my heart starts pumping my fist start pumping," Smith relates the act of falling in love to getting in the boxing ring: that the act of love is a back-and-forth that can be exhaust-ing both physically and mentally. The group reflects the punching that a boxer inflicts by all hitting triplets at the same time on the lyric "upset," which metaphorically "hits" the theme of the song.

Smith follows up with the dreamlike "Distant Fingers," cowritten with Lanier. The song could be viewed as a sister song of sorts to "Birdland" from *Horses* as a deal with God and the quest for a spiritual connection. Smith calls on a higher force to release her from her earthly condition. From the opening lyrics, Smith asks, "When when will you be landing? When when will you return?" This statement evokes the desire of wanting to be taken away to a better place, to be released from and taken from the daily strife of life. Moreover, Smith is beginning to voice her fatigue by speaking of her earthly fantasies crumbling and, upon realizing so, sings, "I'm so tired I quit." This lyrical example of throwing in the towel could speak to the frustration that she felt at the time and just how easy it would have been to just give up.

The tour de force of the record is the album's title track "Radio Ethiopia/Abyssinia." The song was a labor of love for the group, as it attempted several different recordings of the song. Douglas stated, "Patti played guitar on the title tune, which is something nobody else would let her do. She had a Duo-Sonic that was really cool, and she loved to get crazy sounds out of it. We tried the song about four or five times, but we weren't 100 percent happy with it." It wasn't until one dangerous night that Smith decided it was time to record their definitive take on this song. "One night, there was a hurricane [Hurricane Belle], and I told her, 'Do not go out tonight.' But a little while later she called me and said, 'I feel its tonight.' So I drove out in this horrible rain and storm, and we got everybody there, and at about three in the morning, we got it. The track was there, and it sounded terrific. She was feeling it that night."

The track is best described as a ten-minute, noise-laden sonic exploration of the band and its surroundings. Not adhering to any firm harmonic structure, the band is easily able to think outside any framework and instead explore the "voice" of its instrument. The song itself could be likened to a symphony, breaking into three movements with different tempos coming and going as well as different instruments taking center stage. The first movement (roughly 00:00–03:04) begins with a flowing-like guitar effect while the guitar plays a bass-heavy riff and the drums accent the cymbals, creating a disorienting yet exciting pulse. Smith's implementation of slides and auxiliary guitar noise adds to the improvisational aspect of the song, acting as the overture to the improvisational aspects that show themselves throughout the song.

The song's second movement (roughly 03:07–08:30) has the band nearly doubling the tempo while Smith employs vocal affects with barely coherent lyrics that slowly peak their way through the mix of the song. One could explain why her voice was so low in the mix, as it acted as its own improvisational instrument, much like the other members of the ensemble. The last movement of the song (roughly 08:30–10:05) brings the entire feel of the song slowly crashing down in a haze of guitar feedback, vocal moans, and cymbal accents, resulting in a fully concrete artistic expression.

The subsequent track, "Abyssinia," is listed as its own track but is clearly the denouement of "Radio Ethiopia" with the band slowly fading while Smith caps it off by saying, "Every time I see your face I eventually wake up." What is most striking about the song is how many of the aspects that the song utilizes (guitar feedback, vocal embellishments, etc.) have been utilized by the next wave of punk rock/noise rock practitioners. Such bands as Sonic Youth have utilized the same artistic criteria to much critical success and acclaim.

However, the success and acclaim that subsequent practitioners may have experienced were not entirely felt with the release of *Radio Ethiopia*. The album was met with a mixed response from the public and from critics. Some championed the album for its semi-improvisational feel, while others downright hated the lyrics and music. In a particular turn of events, a lot of the critical bashing focused on the band themselves. In his review for *Rolling Stone*, Dave Marsh said, "Her band is basically just another loud punk-rock gang of primitives, riff-based and redundant. The rhythm is disjointed, the guitar chording trite and elementary." This is particularly strange, as the band displayed more than the description that Marsh explains, being anything other than what Marsh describes as "elementary." In her review for *Hit Parader*, Marianne Partridge called the album "an inarticulate mess" and stated that Smith was "into the myth-making business. And in this, her second album, the myth is exposed . . . as cheap thrills." She even calls out Kaye's guitar playing and use of feedback by saying that it was "a mistake, as he consistently bungles it: the secret of feedback lies in knowing how to play a guitar first."

Some critics praised the album for being a fully functioning piece in and of itself outside the influence of *Horses*. Robert Christgau stated for the *Village Voice*, "When it works, which is just about everywhere but the [eleven-minute] title track, this delivers the charge of heavy metal without the depressing predictability." Furthermore, in a revisited review, *Los Angeles Times* critic John Penner spoke of the critical dismay of the record as being a result of bad timing. Penner voiced that the album is great but didn't receive the acclaim that it deserved at the time, as it came right after the insurmountable success of *Horses*. He said, "Add this one to the list with the Velvet Underground's *White Light/White Heat*, The Clash's *Give 'Em Enough Rope* and a number of other great LPs that people had the misfortune to cut right after they cut rock landmarks."

Subsequent reviews of *Radio Ethiopia* reflect the idea that *Horses* catapulted Smith to heights that would make any subsequent record victim of the so-called sophomore slump. In a retroactive review, Kevin Kern of Popstache.com makes the point that most sophomore slumps come from a lack of work ethic or laziness, but *Radio Ethiopia* is neither lazy nor lacking a serious work ethic. Kern states, "Regardless of songwriting credits, what no one wants to hear is a self-professed rebel sounding tired, and despite the album's alleged lack of direction, Smith sounds just as charged-up throughout *Radio Ethiopia* as she does during the best moments of her debut."

The album reached number 122 on the U.S. album charts, reaching its height on January 7, 1977. After the promising start with *Horses*, the commercial and critical reaction to *Radio Ethiopia* was a disappointment to the band and Arista Records. However, the album has found further recognition throughout the years, with time proving its validity. In October 2012, cartoonist and illustrator Charles Burns released the graphic novel *The Hive*, which features a character who is obsessed with *Radio Ethiopia*, as modeled after his former girlfriend's roommate who played the record nonstop upon its release.

The album cover features a relaxed-looking Patti caught midtalking by photographer Lynn Goldsmith. Less confrontational than its predecessor, the cover is more candid yet, perhaps as a result, less stark and bold for an artist who until that time in her career made a point of being so visually and aurally bold. The band continued to be as aurally bold as ever by moving forward and asserting itself into a tour in support of *Radio Ethiopia*. Whether the band failed to communicate its ideas on *Radio Ethiopia* is subject to debate, it cannot be debated that its live shows were continuing to impress fans and critics alike.

After the release of *Radio Ethiopia*, the group held a weeklong residency at the Bottom Line before embarking on a tour with stops in Boston, Cleveland, Milwaukee, Chicago, and several others in the Midwest, ultimately ending the year with a New Year's Eve show at the Palladium in New York. While Smith ended the year on a mixed note— as the resulting reception to *Radio Ethiopia* proved mixed at best—it was the beginning of 1977 that would be the toughest time in her early career.

On January 23, 1977, Smith and the group were opening for Bob Seger in Tampa, Florida, at the Curtis-Hixon Hall when during their performance of "Aint' It Strange," Smith fell off the stage and broke three vertebrae in her neck. Subsequent comments made by Smith target Seeger's road crew as the cause of the accident. Smith told *Uncut Magazine*, "There've been many rumors. . . . 'Oh, she was stoned.' It wasn't like that. I was being careful on the stage because there wasn't as much room or light. I didn't whirl around as much as usual, but when I hit the monitor with my foot, it was half hanging over the lip of the stage."

As a result of the accident, a planned concert at Nassau Coliseum on Long Island and a European tour were canceled. Smith's doctors were quick to suggest that she undergo an operation, which she refused. With a forced sabbatical on her hands and the blessing of Clive Davis to take the time that she needed to recuperate, Smith was free to focus on her next set of poetry. In congruence with this, Smith began to develop material for the group's next album. Smith had begun to read the work of T. E. Lawrence as well as watch the films of Pier Paolo Pasolini, the noted writer and filmmaker. While watching his 1964 film *Il Vangelo secondo Matteo* (*The Gospel According to St. Matthew*), Smith began to admire how the movie told the story of Jesus as a revolutionary figure. This, along with Smith's reading of *The New Testament*, gave her new material a more overtly religious bent.

After several months of recuperation, Smith found herself relying on painkillers to get through the trauma that she sustained in Tampa. Smith's injuries were at one point so severe that she was not able to use the bathroom let alone get out of her bed. To get back into fighting shape, Smith began a series of shows at CBGB as a sort of rock-and-roll physical therapy. The energy of performing invigorated her spirit, as she began the residency by having to be brought out onstage and she ended it without requiring her neck brace.

Beginning work on their third album, *Easter*, Smith and the band enlisted the help of producer Jimmy Iovine, a young up-and-comer whose biggest credits at the time were as an engineer on Bruce Springsteen's *Born to Run* and Meat Loaf's *Bat out of Hell*. Settling into New York's Record Plant studio, the group had the difficult task of trying to build its brand after the negative commercial and critical reception of *Radio Ethiopia*.

Along with the overtly religious title of *Easter*, the album begins with "Till Victory," an up-tempo song where Smith clearly dictates the second coming of Jesus Christ. Smith's overt lyrical content includes lines such as "Rend the veil and we shall sail. The nail, the grail, that's all behind thee," clearly setting the stage of Christ's resurrection. Further-more, the lyric "legions of light virtuous flight ignite, excite. And you will see us coming, V formation through the sky" evokes the feeling of Christ's followers. The lyric "V formation through the sky" may also evoke the band itself. V can be interpreted as the Roman numeral five. Seeing that the Patti Smith Group contained five members, one may make the argument the "V formation" of which she speaks intonates the members of the group seeking to be redeemed after their initial success of *Horses* and the commercial and critical reception of their sophomore slump *Radio Ethiopia*. Smith ends the song by saying to God, "Do not seize me," prompting one to believe that Smith has more to do on this planet before she passes.

"Till Victory" immediately shows the brilliance of Iovine, whose pro-duction value prevents the song from sounding religiously didactic by surrounding the group with an anthemic sound that transcends the lyrical content. With crunchy guitars and heavy drums, the band has never sounded more explicit on any record until this point. Adding layers of dynamic changes creates dramatic sweeps and theatrical arcs that one could say is "Springsteen-esque" in design.

The next song on the record is perhaps the most perplexing of Smith's early career. "Space Monkey" continues with Smith's explora-tion of the extraterrestrial but with at times absurdist/theatrical ele-ments. Additionally, Smith employs a fair amount of vocal embellish-ments and articulations, resulting in several animal-like grunts, squawks, and yelps. The song begins with a Manzarek-esque organ motif, which stays consistent throughout the verses of the song. This connection to the Doors, specifically to Jim Morrison, may have been an influence on Smith's vocal delivery for this piece with her sheer bombast cutting right through the mix.

Lyrically, Smith speaks about her "space monkey" and how it is a contemporary figure, although not of this world. Smith describes it in several ways by singing that the monkey is a "sign on the time-time," "so out of line-line," and "sort of divine." The ultimate identity of the mon-key is up to interpretation. However, in the second stanza of the song, Smith sings "Pierre Clementi. Snortin' cocaine." Smith may be refer-ring to the actor Pierre Clementi, a French star who was arrested in 1972 for possession of cocaine. Clementi's film work often saw him cast in roles where his characters were deemed animalistic in some way or, if not his character, the supporting characters and theme of the movie. One such example is the 1969 film *Pigsty*, where Clementi plays a young man who turns into a cannibal. In the 1974 movie *Steppenwolf*, the plot centers on a man who is half-man/half-animal, with Clementi playing the role of a sensual saxophonist who helps to guide the main character's animalistic desires.

The absurdist elements of this piece reach its pinnacle toward the end when the metaphorical UFO comes to take Smith away. Smith rapidly crescendos the lyrics "Oh, good-bye mama, I'll never do dishes again" while monkey sounds appear in the background, which could easily be interpreted as a sexual climax. The ending reinforces the title of the track, with "space" referring to an unexplored territory and "monkey" symbolizing the animal urges that one has.

Easter is perhaps best known for spawning the top-20 single "Because the Night." Although Smith's antiauthoritarian bent may have proven otherwise, Smith secretly yearned to have a hit song. Not surprising considering the time: Smith came of age in the golden age of radio, when having a hit song meant heavy commercial airplay and an acceptance of sorts. The song was cowritten by fellow New Jersey brethren Bruce Springsteen, and Smith was introduced to it by Iovine, who was friends with Springsteen. At the time, Springsteen was demoing songs that would eventually make up his album *Darkness on the Edge of Town*. In the mix was "Because the Night," an unfinished track that was left out of the album's final lineup. Iovine gave Smith a cassette copy of the track but resisted listening to the song, as the band had already had a cover song ("Privilege") for the record and Smith wanted the remaining tracks to be originals. However, Smith was still recovering from her accident in Tampa, and the band did not have the usual amount of material to record an album. One evening, Smith found the tape and listened to it and was immediately taken by the song's "anthemic quality." Smith then spent the remainder of the night writing the lyrics, which she then presented to the band.

Lyrically, the song is an unconcealed remark on surrendering to love and desire. Smith personifies the intentions of love and lust by using the word "banquet" to describe how palatable love can be. Smith describes love as "an angel, disguised as lust," alluding to the idea that lust is a humanistic trait and love a divine trait. Vocally, Smith incorporates heavy eighth-note syncopation during the bridge, which perfectly represents the ups and downs of love and relationships. The song's most clear indication of love comes in the line "love is a ring, the telephone," eliciting the image of Smith waiting by the telephone for her new love to call—which has a direct line to real events, as the night that Smith wrote the lyrics, she was waiting for Fred to call from Detroit.

"Because the Night" became a radio hit, reaching number 13 on *Billboard Magazine*'s Hot 100 singles chart. However, her core base did not immediately take to the popularity of "Because the Night." Smith later recounted in *New York Magazine* that she was labeled a sellout due to the success of the song. "I liked hearing myself on the radio," she says, with a shrug. "To me, those people didn't understand punk rock at all. Punk rock is just another word for freedom."

In direct opposition of the top-40, power-pop, anthemic declaration that "Because the Night" expressed, "Ghost Dance" has the feeling of a group of friends sitting by the campfire, singing songs and telling stories. Employing only vocals, acoustic guitar, recorder, and auxiliary percussion, the stripped-down instrumentation allows for the lyrics to be delivered in a precise matter, which Iovine augments by having Smith's voice in the front of the mix.

The "Ghost Dance" in question may refer to the Native American practice, a holy tradition meant to reunite the living with the spirits of the departed. The grouplike chant of "We shall live again" that the song employs has an upbeat grace to it, signaling a joyous reunion to come with those who have passed. Furthermore, this reunion will incorporate heavenly gifts, which Smith signifies in the first verse by mentioning "manna from heaven," with "manna" being an edible substance that God gave to the Israelites during their travels in the desert. Smith also signifies eternal peace, which she mentions with the last line "Shake out the ghost," signifying a lack of malice and a desire for spiritual harmony.

Easter also contains one of the most provocative songs to be commercially released and certainly the most controversial one in Smith's catalog. "Rock and Roll Nigger" brilliantly employs the hateful word as a means of describing anyone attempting to do something outside of contemporary society or against the norms of authority. Smith exclaims, "Outside of society that's where I want to be," which delves into Smith's artistic thought process and how she wishes to be viewed as an individual.

Throughout the song, Smith contextualizes what she means by the word "nigger" and how it pertains to society. First, she alludes to herself as a nigger by stating, "Baby was a black sheep, baby was a whore. Baby got big and baby get bigger," which could refer to her first pregnancy and how society views her for her decision to give her baby up for adoption. The song itself was clearly arranged so that the lyrics are explicit and out in the open, with the accompaniment playing a straight-ahead rock progression. "Rock and Roll Nigger" is a clear indication about the importance of lyrical recitation in popular music and the weight of lyrical content. Smith sings the first verse, where she describes herself before Lenny Kaye sings the second verse. This creates a subtle but intelligent subtext to the song as a whole. Historically speaking, women have been kept on the fringe of society, and white men have been the dominant political and historical force. By having Kaye sing the second verse, Smith is using his voice as a way of offering insight into the perspective of a white person in a contemporary society: that Kaye, as a white man, could be subject to injustice just like anyone else.

In a 1978 article with *Rolling Stone*, Smith stated, "I redefine the word *nigger* as being an artist-mutant that was going beyond gender." With this quote, Smith is attempting to meld her status as a sexual and artistic iconoclast among her contemporary music peers. For a white woman, the sheer audacity of saying that she wants to redefine the word "nigger" is positive as well as beyond her means. At the same time, she is actively pointing her finger toward the establishment with the lyric "Oh look around you, all around you riding on a copper wave." The "copper wave" in question may be in reference to copper being used as a synonym to riches, as copper was one of the first metals to be used to make jewelry, which in turn would be used to show the wealth of a particular person or group. Smith may also be using copper as a means of calling out the working class, as tools are often made of copper.

Critics were one to assert the notion that she clearly did not know the connotation of the word "nigger." Critic Dave Marsh spoke of the word's usage by stating, "Smith doesn't understand the word's connotation, which is not outlawry but a particular kind of subjugation and humiliation that's antithetical to her motives." I make the argument that Smith was trying to reaffirm that word by placing it in the positive instead, a practice sometimes used among African Americans. This is supported later in the song where she runs of a list of names that she truly admires and calls them "niggers." She exclaims, "Jimi Hendrix was a nigger. Jesus and grandma too. Jackson Pollock was a nigger." All were artists who, at certain times in their artistic pursuits, were seen as being outside the norms of society.

On the second side of the album, the group includes a cover of the song "Privilege (Set Me Free)." Written by Mel London and Mike Leander, the song was created for the 1967 movie *Privilege*, which tells the story of a pop singer who is sought by the church and state of a futuristic society with the sole purpose of turning him into a savior of the people. The movie is riddled with exaggerated religious iconography as well as the popular culture of the 1960s in an exaggerated dystopia that plays out as part satire and part mockumentary.

The original version of the song plays in the movie when the character Steven Shorter is being led in a metal cage on a stage while cops harass him. The scene is meant to be carefully choreographed for the audience to elicit a response, in a similar fashion to what James Brown would do in front of audiences by feigning being hurt for a dramatic effect. In the original, London and Leander create a dreamlike atmosphere with robust-sounding drums and creepy choral effects. For their cover, Smith and the group maintain a lot of the same effects, especially with the organlike effects.

The choice of this song may be foreshadowing what was to come of Smith, who would later retire after the group's fourth album, becoming disillusioned with her career. The lyrics are laden with clues regarding her feelings about rock and roll. Smith opens the verse by stating, "I see it all before me, the days of love and torment. The nights of rock and roll, I see it all before me," which reflects her seeing how her future will play out: another stop on a tour, fans fawning over her without feeling happiness. Furthermore, Smith gives several other examples of her disillusionment by stating, "Sometimes my spirit's empty" and "Oh, God, give me something, a reason to live"—both lyrics reflecting the void that Smith was experiencing even with a successful career.

Additionally, the scene in *Privilege* where this takes place is on a concert stage, which can be seen as a direct correlation between what the character felt in the movie and what Smith felt at the time. Within this scene in the movie, Shorter is being depicted as a Christ-like figure with an excited, if not downright hysterical, audience screaming and reaching out to him. Before and after the release of *Easter,* one could make the case that Smith was at the apex of her popularity with similar audiences wanting any bit of her. The Christlike allegory is heightened in Smith's version of the song where she incorporates Psalm 23 from the bible. Smith does this in a spoken word by stating, "The Lord is my shepherd, I shall not want. He maketh me to lie down in green pastures." She later speaks the lines "Yeah, though I walk through the valley of the shadow of death. I will fear no evil for Thou art with me." Incorporating this psalm is a direct through line saying that Smith is keeping God by her side as she continues her rise to fame.

The album's most beautiful track may be "We Three," which tells the story of an ménage a trois of sorts. The music is framed in a rather cinematic way with the 1960s girl group–esque arrangement evoking a scenario of Smith walking along the street, singing the lyrics into a fictitional movie camera, telling the audience of her sordid story. While the vocal attack that Smith employed throughout her career was generated from her throat, "We Three" contains an almost operatic timbre, which she executes by singing more from her diaphragm. This creates a beautiful sense of longing, which, coupled with the arpeggiated waltz of the piano, enhances the mood of the song.

The song's ambiguity of who the "three" are leaves the song open to interpretation. One such interpretation is the three are Smith, Mapplethorpe, and Jim Carroll, who all lived together for a period. Smith calls out how the relationship among the three of them is fragile by crooning, "Oh, the dice roll so deceptively for we three." The fragility in question could refer to the drug problems that Mapplethorpe and Carroll were dealing with at the time, adding the smell of tragedy to the song. Smith pours her heart into the lyric "You said when you were with me that nothing made you high," adding the idea that Smith herself was the drug, the muse to their creativity.

An additional rumor, one that is more popular, is that it revolved around Tom Verlaine of Television and Allen Lanier of Blue Oyster Cult, whom Smith was dating at the same time. This idea is ultimately supported by the fact that Smith wrote this song with Verlaine and would have had a more direct emotional acuity with the details at hand. Additionally, the ambiguity of the song could be used as a metaphor for any grouping of people in her life at the time. The opening line, of which Smith speaks, is "Every Sunday, I would go down to the bar where he played guitar." The bar in question could easily be CBGB, whose revolving cast of characters could have easily taken any spot within the song.

Smith follows with "25th Floor" and its companion piece "High on Rebellion." "25th Floor" begins with a confident guitar riff that you can see inciting a sneer on Smith's face. The title of the song alludes to the floor where Patti and Fred partied on the night they met. Metaphorically, "The 25th Floor" could also mean a height of success or a goal that Smith was trying to reach. The introduction guitar riff supports the confident performance of Smith, who speaks about sexual desire and the exploration of love and lust. Smith begins the verse by stating, "We explore the men's room, we don't give a shit," which alludes to the idea that Patti and women in general are beginning to venture into areas that at one time were available only to men. The next lyric describes the women's room as lacking electricity and that she takes "vows inside of it," resulting in the concept that she is looking to make a promise to herself to continue to explore and expand as a performer.

Smith continues her metaphorical desire to explore new destinations by singing, "Desire to dance, too startled to try, wrap my legs around you, starting to fly," which paints this picture that what she is seeing or experiencing for the first time frightens her in a way but she has no eagerness to look back, only to move forward to the highest pinnacle she can possibly reach. "The 25th Floor" technically concludes with the song "High on Rebellion," which could better be described as a coda, with Smith improvising lyrics about the powers of her guitar and how rebellion gives her a euphoric feeling. The lyrics mirror some of the content that Smith originally spoke about in "The 25th Floor." Smith begins by stating, "What I feel when I'm playing guitar is completely cold and crazy, like I don't owe nobody nothing and it's just a test just to see how far I can relax into the cold wave of a note." Smith is positing that when she plays guitar, it's a battle of sorts between the guitar and herself. If the guitar wins, Smith becomes more "crazy." If she wins, she reaches a pure state of euphoria. The band tries to mirror the "cold and crazy" element of the lyrics by not improvising per se but rather musically free associating on the song's form. Kaye especially achieves this toward the end of the song by tremolo picking on the guitar's higher strings and rapidly going up its neck creating a fervent, manic sound.

The group ends the album on a somber, however powerful, note. The album's title track caps the album's religious overtones by incorporating sounds that one would associate with a funeral: organ, bells, and bagpipes. First, the use of the organ calls on a sense of loss, a period of morning. Second, the use of church bells reinforces the idea that once they are struck, the Lord's Prayer must be recited. Last, the use of bagpipes calls on the idea that a death has occurred, given how they are used in Irish funerals and services. During verses where Smith speaks of "Isabella," Kaye's guitar doubles her vocal line. While this was most likely employed to support the melody and make it appear more robust, metaphorically it could mean that Kaye is trying to physically support her to avoid falling into the mix.

"Isabella," as well as "Frederic" and "Vitalie," that she speaks of could refer to Rimabaud's progeny: Jean Nicolas Frédéric, Jeanne-Rosalie-Vitalie, and Frédérique Marie Isabelle. "Isabelle" may also refer to Rimabud's sister, who was present at the time of Rimbaud's death from what was believed to be cancer. This assertion is supported by Smith upon singing, "Isabella, we are dying. Isabella, we are rising," possibly taking the voice of Rimbaud and describing his ascent into Heaven. The song ends on a haunting note with a choir of women chanting "Isabella, we are rising," providing a solemn end to an album rife with religious arcs.

Whereas *Radio Ethiopia* polarized critics, *Easter* was received with a more positive reaction. Daisann McLane in *Crawdaddy* magazine stated, "Musically, this is Smith's best album. What was implied on *Horses* is filled in on *Easter*, and improved." Nick Tosches in *Creem* magazine echoed this by stating, "Truer and surer and less uneven than her previous albums, *Easter* is Smith's best work." Chris Brazier in his review for *Melody Maker* perhaps gave the most backhanded compliment by stating, "I'm not happy about evaluating a Patti Smith album in a matter of hours, remembering the time I took loving and learning with *Horses*, but I reckon this is a distinct improvement on *Radio Ethiopia*, which nevertheless falls short of the glorious heights of which she is capable."

Whatever "glorious heights" Brazier spoke of manifested itself in a positive way, as *Easter* gave Smith the hit song that she wanted with "Because the Night" and the album itself reached number 20 on *Billboard Magazine*'s Hot 100. *Easter* continued to draw on Smith's adventurous spirit and the way that she would roll the dice with her career. In a January 2012 interview for *New York Magazine*, Smith stated, "I made a lot of decisions that affected my success, I know that." "I wouldn't go on Dick Clark because I'd be required to lip-synch. I showed armpit hair on the cover of my Easter album, and it was so disturbing to people, which I still don't understand, so they wouldn't rack it in the South. Then other people wouldn't rack it because I had a song called 'Rock and Roll Nigger.'"

This lack of compromise and ability to circumvent authority is reflected on the album's cover. The cover depicts the concept of encountering Smith in a private moment as she looks down toward the ground as her arms are raised about her head with her hands in her hair. Have we interrupted Smith fixing her hair? Are her pursed lips supposed to denote that she was saying something or possibly singing? Smith's raised arms show a smattering of dark armpit hair, which is made all the more apparent with her fair skin and stunningly white blouse. The cover encapsulates the free spirit and empowered nature of Smith and the album itself. Smith not looking into the camera represents her desire of eschewing the world around her through a portal that extols the components of being a contemporary woman that does not need to be analyzed or defined within the confines of modern society.

By this time in Smith's career, her visual presence had become a mainstay of television and print. The same year that *Easter* was released, Smith released a book of poetry titled *Babel*. To promote her book, Smith appeared on *The Mike Douglas Show* on March 8, 1978. Appearing alongside comedians Jerry Stiller and Anne Meara, actress Kristy McNichol, and actor William Shatner, Douglas does not spend any time talking about *Babel* but rather spoke mostly about Smith's "punk" appearance (even though what she was wearing was not even "punk"—a green blouse, gray vest, and orange pants). The majority of the interview is spent speaking about Muhammad Ali, specifically about his match with Leon Spinks at the Superdome in New Orleans, which happened the previous month on February 15, 1978. The match had been considered controversial, as Spinks was named the victor after a fifteen-round bout, without knocking out Ali. Smith's take on the match spoke volumes about her feelings toward being a champion. Smith said of Ali, "As far as I'm concerned he's still champ because I believe that a champ is a champ until somebody knocks him to the ground."

Perhaps as a sign of approval by the popular masses, *Saturday Night Live* aired a sketch on its December 9, 1978, broadcast featuring a sketch titled "Candy Slice." In it, Gilda Radnor's look is reminiscent of Smith's: long stringy hair with a white shirt and black pants. The portrayal of the character could be seen as unflattering, with Candy Slice falling in and out of consciousness during a studio session and having to be propped up and kept alert by various crew members. The sketch represented the generalized pop culture perception of Patti Smith and other female punk rockers of the time. Another reading was that the show used Smith and the character of Candy Slice as a device for the empty-headedness that the 1970s popular music scene was creating at the time.

Candy Slice proved to be popular and was subsequently brought back on a broadcast on February 17, 1979. As part of a fictional benefit concert entitled "Rock against Yeast '79," Radnor sang a song entitled "Gimme Mick," which sees Candy Slice singing about the androgynous qualities that both Smith and Jagger felt at this time. During the verse, Slice sings, "Baby's hair, bulgin' eyes, lips so thick, are you a woman? Are you a man? I'm your biggest funked-up fan!" During the bridge, Candy—having confessed her attraction to Mick—launches into a Smith-esque stream of consciousness that is both humorous and a tribute of sorts to Smith.

With popular culture assigning Patti as its punk rock signifier, the weight of such an assignment would prove to be too much as the 1970s rolled to a close.

5

"SO YOU WANT TO BE A ROCK 'N' ROLL STAR?"

1978–1986

As the 1970s drew to a close, the world at large was trying to move on from indiscretions of the past by placing historical Band-Aids on the generation's major cultural events. On January 4, 1979, the state of Ohio paid $675,000 to the families of those who were killed or injured during the Kent State University shootings that occurred on May 4, 1970. On February 2, 1979, the Sex Pistols bassist Sid Vicious overdosed on heroin following his incarceration for attempted murder of his girlfriend Nancy Spungeon at the Hotel Chelsea, ultimately sealing his fate as punk rock's nihilistic James Dean and pulling the brakes on punk rock's first wave.

Set to the tunes of hit songs such as the Village People's "YMCA" and Rod Stewart's "Do Ya Think I'm Sexy," the popular music scene of this time was winding down from the top-40 anthems of the decade and the virus of disco fever, allowing a new generation of rock-and-roll acts to begin their journey—all of this as Smith was winding down from the first part of her career.

The success of "Because the Night" launched the group from the niche New York City punk rock cosmos into mainstream acceptance. Upon the release of *Easter*, the group embarked on a breakneck European tour, with stops in Norway, Sweden, Denmark, Germany, France, and England. While in England, the group taped appearances on two

British mainstays, with each showing a different side of Patti and how media was looking to sell her to the British people. On April 1, 1978, the group performed on the ITV program *The South Bank Show*, a popular culture-and-arts television magazine. The program aimed to look at how rock and roll had evolved, with Smith representing the new generation and with a segment with rock-and-roll pioneer Carl Perkins representing the older guard.

Host Melvyn Bragg juxtaposes Perkins's contributions to rock and roll and Smith's adherence to rock and roll as a lifestyle, stating that "Patti Smith is the next generation which adopted rock and roll not only for its music but as a way of living. It formed people's thoughts about society and to have a style that attracted writers, artists and all sorts of enthusiasts." Bragg then finishes his introduction with a hefty conclusion: "Patti Smith is an evangelist for the music and for the way of life."

During her interview, Smith offers her insights on the current state of rock and roll and the discourse that surrounds it. Smith declared, "Rock and roll is the most universal tongue we have available to us now and I think if someone is going to sell five million records they should be saying something within those five million records." Smith parses the responsibility of rock and roll and those who practice it as their art and perhaps surmises the record industry as a whole by asserting, "Most people that are selling that many records right now aren't doing anything really to communicate. . . . They're just taking people's money and giving them sort of mediocre entertainment in exchange."

Showing a clear difference between American and European media and what is acceptable for broadcast, the group performed a rousing rendition of "Rock and Roll Nigger." In the introduction of the song, Patti recites a poem and mentions, "In heart, I am an American artist and I have no guilt. I seek pleasure, I seek the nerves under your skin the narrow archway," offering the righteous exclamation that she will not be hushed or silenced as an artist. She concludes her decree by stating, "I have not sold my soul to God!" and dramatically throws her notebook to the floor. This unbridled performance shows an angrier persona of Smith and a side of her that is not willing to take it anymore.

After the performance, Bragg speaks to music critic Paul Gambaccini, who parses that "Rock and Roll Nigger" is a calculated title and that he would not expect the more acceptable title "Rock and Roll Negro" or any variant coming from Patti Smith. In contrast with her performance on *The South Bank Show*, Smith's performance of "Because the Night" and "The 25th Floor" on *The Old Grey Whistle Test* showed that a more reserved persona didn't provoke as much as sell "Because the Night" as a hit single.

After their European tour, Smith and the band spent April through August on an American tour before returning to Europe for a series of performances in the United Kingdom, Germany, and Austria. The group ended the year with a residency at CBGB before beginning work on its fourth album. At the helm of what would become the album *Wave*, Smith enlisted the help of producer/musician and friend Todd Rundgren. At this point in his career, Rundgren had proven himself to be a venerable force as both a musician and a producer. As a solo artist, Rundgren had several releases under his belt, including 1970's *Runt*, 1972's *Something/Anything*, and 1974's *Todd*. As a producer, Rundgren was coming off of the unprecedented success of singer Meatloaf's *Bat out of Hell*, which spawned the hit songs "You Took the Words Right out of My Mouth (Hot Summer Night)" and "Paradise by the Dashboard Light" and sold 14,000,000 in the United States alone.

Rundgren was especially attracted to Smith's performance style and the arc of her technique that she applied to her performances. Rundgren stated, "I was fascinated with the intensity of her performance. She would go off into these improvisations and it was just incredibly intense, for a single person, the way she captured the audience and took them through all these various facets of her personality."

Settling into Bearsville Studios in Woodstock, New York, the sessions for *Wave* went smoothly, which Daugherty partially attributed to Rundgren's facilities as a musician as well as his shorthand with the recording console at Bearsville. Additionally, the sessions were aided by Rundgren's success at blending all the group members' personalities into one cohesive unit. Smith stated, "[Rundgren] didn't take me aside and cut me off from the band. So many producers will try to triangulate, or they have some drummer who's always better than your guy or something. But I wanted people to know that, if they bought a record that was supposed to the Patti Smith Group, then that's what they heard."

The album begins with the song "Frederick," an upbeat love song dedicated to Fred "Sonic" Smith. Smith stated that the impetus of the song came to her while walking on the beach trying to think of ideas for *Wave*. Not having a firm idea of what it should sound like, all that Smith could surmise was that she wanted the result to be "so happy and accessible that everybody would want to dance." Rundgren replied to Smith's request for a danceable song with a disco-esque drumbeat during the verses and oscillating piano tones, sounding prime for 1970s radio airplay.

Aiding in the danceability of the song is Rundgren's manipulation of Smith's voice, which he used to build multipart harmonies throughout the song. Smith at the time still did not see herself as a bonafide singer, which caused her to feel anxiety in the studio while recording "Frederick." Smith recounted, "I can sing but, especially at that time in my life, I was more of a 'performance singer' and I didn't have that much training." Although the results are satisfactory, Smith ultimately stated, "[It was] hell for me, because I don't hear harmonies, and feel silly doing falsetto. I couldn't imagine how these voices would translate, because I don't have the aural vision that Todd has."

In keeping with the ongoing device of expressing love through religious imagery, Smith's use of the lyric "Tonight on the wings of a dove, up above to the land of love" juxtaposes the innocent sincerity of being deeply and passionately in love with the pursuit of a deeper meaning of love. The polished production value of this song and *Wave* as a whole could lead an ardent fan of the group's previous three albums to question its artistic candor. However, "Frederick" is a great example of Smith shedding her signature conformational style and instead applying a more lyrically explicit inflection to better serve the song's theme.

Immediately with "Frederick," Smith shows a less confrontational character and is seemingly ready to move on. On *Horses, Radio Ethiopia,* and *Easter,* Smith incorporated metaphor, religious imagery, and other devices. *Wave* sees more of Smith stripping away those devices and revealing a new skin. Although she does continue to use poetic mechanisms and lyrical conventions to reveal herself on *Wave,* Smith's cutting back on said devices opens up the music to tell more of the story. Furthermore, this stripping away of past experiences and hardships is a brave new frontier for Smith, letting Rundgren sonically lead the band to uncharted territory.

Musically, "Frederick" could be seen as the musical sister to Springsteen's "Prove It All Night," as both utilize a similar piano introduction. Several critics also purported that "Frederick" sounded just like "Because the Night," which Smith would often express disdain for. Telling

New York Rocker, Smith stated, "I was playing ["Frederick"] once on the piano, and it did sound a little like 'Because The Night,' but that's only because it has the same basic chord structure. Big deal—'Prove It All Night' sounds like a dozen other songs, how many new chord combinations can you come up with? To me, 'Frederick' sounds more like a Motown song. We never intended to capitalize on any similarities; purely incidental."

A direct antithesis of the Motown sound that Smith may have aimed for with "Frederick," the subsequent song "Dancing Barefoot" has a light, ethereal quality where Smith tells a story using the personal pronouns "she" and "he" and the addictive quality of being in love. In its most simple idea, the "she" and "he" in question could be swapped for Patti and Fred, whom she also dedicated this song to. "Dancing Barefoot" quickly changes the mood set by "Frederick" with an acoustic guitar playing E Minor, D Major, E Minor, A Major, setting the minor key verses that Smith mirrors with her soft-spoken vocal delivery, summoning a Morrison-esque quality that gives the song a hypnotic, otherworldly feel. The vocal delivery is noteworthy, with the verses being sung in a masculine way and the choruses being performing in a higher, feminine register, creating a timbral duality.

Cowritten with Kral, the music came from a cassette that Kral had of several loose ideas, and it was one of the final songs to be recorded. Starting with the acoustic guitar riff, Smith and Kral brought the loosely arranged song to the band to develop. "Dancing Barefoot" shows Rundgren's capacities to build large guitar and keyboard textures without sullying the aural experience of the song at hand. Lyrically, Smith is speaking about true love and when it hits an individual, it takes the person over. Smith supports this with the lyrics, "Here I go and I don't know why, I feel so ceaselessly," which evokes the notion that love controls the individual, not vice versa. The idea of "love" about which the songs speaks has a dual meeting: on one hand, it speaks quite obviously about the love between two people; on the other, it speaks of a love between a person and one's God or spiritual beliefs.

"Dancing Barefoot" also plays into the idea of what one will do while under the guise of love. In the liner notes of the album, Smith dedicated "Dancing Barefoot" to Jeanne Hebuterne, the common-law wife of Parisian artist Amedeo Modigliani. Upon their meeting, Hebuterne became the artistic focus of his work, which resulted in several pieces, such as *Hébuterne* (1918) and *Jeanne Hebuterne (Au chapeau)* (1919), to name a few. Grief stricken after the death of Modigliani on January 24, 1920, Hebuterne committed suicide by jumping out the fifth-floor window of her parents' home, killing both herself and her unborn child.

"Dancing Barefoot" has gone on to have a life of its own following the release of *Wave*. The song has been covered numerous times by everyone from U2 and Pearl Jam to Simple Minds and Allison Moorer. In 2004, *Rolling Stone* listed the song as number 331 on its list of the 500 Greatest Songs of All Time." Even Rundgren himself recorded an arrangement of the song for his 2011 album *(re)Production*.

A highlight of the album is Smith's interpretation of the song "So You Want to Be a Rock 'n' Roll Star," originally recorded by the Byrds. Written by Jim McGuinn and Chris Hillman, the duo wrote the song in response to the creation of the made-for-television musical act *The Monkees*. The resulting success of *The Monkees* caused McGuinn and Hillman to take a step back and view how manufactured rock-and-roll music had become at that point. Smith first heard the song years before via her friend Ed Hansen, who gave her the record and told her, "This song is going to be important to you." The song appears to be the perfect vessel for Smith's dissatisfaction with the popular music industry. The lyrics clearly dictate how a person can become a rock-and-roll star by getting "an electric guitar and take some time and learn how to play. And when your hair's combed right and your pants are tight, it's gonna be all right." The lyrics explicitly speak that image and talent are one and the same, which Smith could easily relate to, as her image and music were so closely tied together.

Whereas the original had a tongue-in-cheek delivery, Smith's interpretation of "So You Want to Be a Rock 'n' Roll Star" is more biting and forceful. The original's genial arrangement seemingly welcomes a person to become a rock-and-roll star with its squeaky-clean delivery and polished prose. Smith's arrangement is more confrontational, insisting that the listener become a rock-and-roll star and a puppet to the masses. This is reflected in the additional verse that Smith includes: "Hey you, come here! Get up! Ah, this is the era where everybody creates!" She becomes the character of a corporate stooge by demanding that you create for monetary gains to occur. The group is at its most comfortable on *Wave* with its interpretation of "So You Want to Be a Rock 'n' Roll Star." Loose but not sloppy, tight but not stringent, the group sticks close to the original while providing a freewheeling feel that Smith playfully fools around with.

"Hymn" could easily be defined as the most calculated song on *Wave*. Clocking in at 1:12, the track serves as a palette cleanser before the end of the first side of the album. Smith's vocal delivery is that of an earnest, Bible-carrying parishioner, quivering at the thought of delivering praise to her God. The line "to take his hand, his sacred heart" is delivered with such emotion that you can picture a group of people coming together and singing this song during a Sunday service.

Smith holds back her Jersey drawl at certain moments during "Hymn" as if to make sure that she annunciates the words clearly, to not offend or be disrespectful. As a result, the song feels more like an etude than lullaby, offering the listener more a display of Smith's technique than a narrative. The way that she sings the word "comfort" in the line "He comes to comfort me" is rounded with no hint of an accent or inflection. The sparse instrumentation and the mix allow for Patti's vocal to be right up front, as if you were dead center in the middle of her musical congregation.

The first side of *Wave* closes with the song "Revenge," a jilted damnation of love gone wrong. Until this point, Smith had carried the album on a "wave" of love songs—with "Frederick" as a declaration of love to Fred, "Dancing Barefoot" as a cautionary tale about the power of love, and "Hymn" as a song in praise of spiritual affection. "Revenge" offers a musical personification of dealing with a breakup. The eerily familiar opening guitar riff evokes the arpeggiated guitar introduction of the Beatles' "I Want You," setting up the minor key feel and ending the first side of the album on a timbrally different texture.

Smith uses the verses to slowly turn up her anger, like a deserted lover waiting a turn to get back at the person who has done wrong. Smith carries the verses in a rational, straight-ahead fashion, declaring, "I thought you were some perfect readout, some digital delay had obscured and phased my view," with "digital delay" perhaps taking the place of love and how it blinds people into not truly seeing people for who they really are. The choruses start when Smith and the band let loose to express the dismay that this lover feels. The piano plays a triplet feel, which evokes this pulse of feet walking away or, in a more aggressive notion, a violent act.

Smith describes the angry tone of the lyrics as a way of offsetting the dark tone of the music. Smith stated, "Lyrically, it's from a very strong female point of view. It's sort of my song encoding anybody that fucked with me; especially all males who had messed with me. It was like 'Fuck you!' because I had Fred and nobody could touch me now."

Wave features a fair amount of material from Ivan Kral, with the song "Citizen Ship" perfectly showcasing his best compositional efforts for the album. The song can be seen as a thinly veiled indictment of refugees and their assimilation into America. This is perhaps due to Kral's refugee-like status, with his possible recollection of Soviet-era ideas through the track's opening line "It didn't matter to me, there were tanks all over my city. There was water outside the windows and children in the streets were throwing rocks at tanks." "Citizen Ship" plays off the concept of citizenship dictating your identity and ultimately your freedom. Smith's sarcastic delivery of the line "Lose your grip on the citizen ship you're cast you're cast away" evokes the idea that a lack of citizenship will ultimately leave you a man without a land and fundamentally lost in the vast sea of life.

"Seven Ways of Going" may very well be the most abstract piece on *Wave* and the most misunderstood piece on the record. Smith evokes biblical themes by saturating the lyrical content of the song with "seven," an obvious and calculated ode to the numerous uses of seven in the Bible, especially in the Book of Revelations, which explains that there are seven churches, seven spirits, seven stars, and so on. More so than a formal ode to the Bible, the use of seven has a deeper meaning to Smith's life at this time, as this would be her final album for close to ten years. Leviticus 23:15–16 states, "From the day after the Sabbath, the day you brought the sheaf of the wave offering, count off seven full weeks. Count off fifty days up to the day after the seventh Sabbath, and then present an offering of new grain to the Lord." This passage speaks of "seven" meaning a sense of completion; that is, Smith may have been trying to convey with this album that, musically, she was complete. Smith uses the "Seven Ways of Going" to praise God for helping her see the "everlasting light" as well as voice her past "sins." The line "Lord, I do extol thee for thou hast lifted me, woke me up and shook me out of mine iniquity for I was undulating in the lewd impostered night" carries the thought that Smith was moving about her life in a smooth fashion toward a life that was under an assumed identity.

Musically, the abstract nature of the quality is more akin to modal jazz than to popular music or rock music. Essentially, the group vamps over a F-7 chord, with Sohl repeating F, C, and Eb for most of the song, allowing free improvisation to occur. This is of particular note when the group performed the song on the West German television program *Rockpalat* on April 21, 1979. During the group's performance of "Seven Ways of Going," Smith improvises on the clarinet, at times calling on free jazz elements that John Coltrane would employ. Coltrane in his late career was trying to reach spiritual levels of performance through free improvisational practices and abstract musical devices, which Smith appears to be reaching. As a result, the group throws a musical wrench into the expectation of the listeners and broadens their musical scope by incorporating aural techniques outside the spectrum of rock and roll.

"Broken Flag" takes *Wave* to a melancholy place with its slow, piano-drenched declaration of sacrificing one's self for the sake of a higher cause. In the liner notes, Smith dedicated the song to Barbara Fritchie, a woman who at the age of ninety-five, in an attempt to block the oncoming Confederate soldiers during the Civil War, waved a Union flag in the middle of the street in Frederick, Maryland. Accounts of what actually happened or even if it ever happened are subject to debate; however, the incident did result in a famous poem written by John Greenleaf Whittier in 1964.

Less so whether the incident occurred or not, the flag is seen as a symbol of standing up for one's beliefs and journeying toward a new life. The new life that Smith was conveying was the life that she was about to embark on with Fred, outside the spotlight. However, the emotional delivery by Smith conveys a mournful tone as opposed to a happy one. The way that she sings "The sifting cloth is binding and the dream she weaves will never end" presents the idea that she will always continue to work creatively toward a never-ending goal.

If "Broken Flag" elicited the idea that the goal will always continue, then the album's title track sends a clear signal that Smith is leaving and not looking back. It was the culmination of an album that explicitly stated that Smith was due to start a new life outside the band. The sparse instrumentation of voice, cello, and piano set to the swooshing sounds of a wave that was programmed on a Moog synthesizer is both haunting and beautiful. Musically, the addition of Kral on cello is what gave the track its most haunting feeling, with his performance mirroring the vocal inflections of Tibetan throat singers, resulting in more of a choirlike sound as opposed to a purely singular instrumental sound. It conjures up the idea that Smith is speaking to someone during a religious service and is trying to unburden herself or seek guidance through her faith.

Smith begins the song with a gentle, childlike spoken-word "Hi, hi," giving off the notion that what she is going to say subsequent to this may be said in a nervous, not completely believed-in matter. The song is a thinly veiled, one-sided conversation between Smith and Pope John Paul I, who is waving to a crowd, of which Smith is hypothetically a member. Smith spoke of her love for Pope John Paul I, who had recently passed away, by stating, "He was just such a pastoral, beautiful man and he had died so quickly. I really believed that he would have been a revolutionary Pope, had he lived."

For the title track, Smith produced the sessions herself with one of the studio's house engineers while Rundgren went to Chicago to perform. Smith enjoyed the complete freedom and later stated, "It was the first time that I'd been alone in the studio and given complete control." Smith began with the piano part and slowly began to incorporate the rest of the band into the mix, asking each member to accomplish a specific task. Upon completion of the session, Smith mixed the track with the engineer, shutting the door on this part of her life by gently whispering at the end of the song, "Wave to the children, wave goodbye."

Released on May 17, 1979, *Wave* received consistent positive and negative responses, although it appeared to lean more toward the latter. Reaching number 18 on *Billboard Magazine*'s Top 200, critics still felt the need to compare her latest work to her previous work. *Rolling Stone*'s Tom Carson, while praising Smith as an artist in the beginning of his review, felt that the album ultimately falls short especially in comparison to her previous work. Carson stated, "Though a long way from being a total disaster, *Wave* is too confused and hermetically smug to be much more than an interesting failure. Simultaneously overworked and unfelt, it's a transitional album in the most transient sense of the word."

Simon Frith of *Melody Maker* mirrors this idea of *Wave* being a transitional record, or an intermediary record. While Frith champions the group's cover of "So You Want to Be a Rock 'n' Roll Star," he deduces that Smith's rock-and-roll fandom has permeated her music with mixed results. Frith stated, "Patti Smith's problem is that what was touching in a rock fan is obnoxious in a rock star. Her desperate faith in the cleansing spiritual power of rock 'n' roll was inspiring as long as she was on the outside." Furthermore, Frith stated, "Unfortunately, inevitably, once Patti had made it—long term contract, rave reviews—she became, given her belief in rock stars as shamans, her own myth." Frith's notion—that once Smith had broken through to the inside of the rock-and-roll business, she became the very myth that she had come to worship before her success—is heavy-handed and voices the opinion of the type of fan who wishes that she had stayed small time and loathes her for seeking success.

Robert Christgau was fair with the material and called out the idea that people had it out for her because of her desire for more mainstream acceptance. Christgau states, "A lot of folks just don't like Patti anymore." Christgau further supports the album by stating, "This is an often inspired album, quirkier than the more generally satisfying *Easter*—especially on the sexual mystery song 'Dancing Barefoot,' quite possibly her greatest track ever."

As the last album during this time in her creative life, Smith recalls fond memories of making *Wave* but was clearly emotionally and physically exhausted with the rock-and-roll machine and the constant recording and performing. Smith later stated, "I felt that I had reached a wall and needed to replenish, learn more and study more. I just didn't' think I had anything more to give people until I learned more about myself." *Wave* ultimately represented the long end of a journey for Patti. Patti later said "It's funny, but before we were recording *Horses*, I never really thought I would ever even make one record. It was never one of my dreams. I just wanted to be an artist or to write a book or something. Then, they asked me to do more records until, by the time of *Wave*, I felt that I couldn't possibly have any more to contribute. And probably, at that time, it was everything that I knew or had to say."

The album cover for *Wave* was something of a full-circle decision as well. Shot by Mapplethorpe in the same room that the cover photo of *Horses* was shot, the photo depicts Smith staring right into the lens with an intense glare while light hits her white dress, creating a calm atmosphere. A tree obscures part of her left arm while she holds two doves resting on both her hands, perhaps representing a part of her life that she is ready to let go of and let simply fly away.

Following the release of *Wave*, the group went on an extensive American tour. In the summer of 1979, the Patti Smith Group performed a few select European dates, with France, Holland, England, Germany, and Italy as part of its itinerary. The group's final date was in Florence, Italy, at the Stadio Comunale, a football stadium built in 1931 with a capacity of 47,290. The group ended its set with a frenetic rendition of "My Generation," which served as a capstone to a decade where Patti Smith the person met Patti Smith the artist. This was to be the last time that Patti Smith performed a complete set in almost fourteen years.

The dissolution of the band proved to come out of nowhere for some of the members, while others saw it coming a mile away. In a 1986 interview for MTV, Kral stated that he did not see it coming: "I really don't know why we broke up. I guess Patti had it. After four albums and playing one of the biggest places in Milan she decided it was time to quit. She broke up at the time that I least expected that. Either she was exhausted or she exhausted her artistic possibilities and she just wanted to stop altogether." Kaye has a more tactful telling of the events surrounding the breakup by mentioning, "It was increasingly apparent that, in a certain sense that we had run our course in that configuration. On that last tour, we were playing all of the great venues, like the Winterland in San Francisco or the Palladium in New York. We were riding a wave, but there was nothing left to say."

In the spring of 1979, Fred and Patti moved to Detroit to begin their new lives together. For a period, Fred and Patti lived in the Book Cadillac, a historic hotel in downtown Detroit where all they had was his guitars as well as Patti's clarinet and favorite books. Soon after, Fred and Patti moved into a home in the suburb of Lake Saint Clair. Fred and Patti married on March 1, 1980, in Detroit in an intimate ceremony that was attended by only their parents. Although the burnout from constant writing, recording, and touring had finally taken its toll, Smith found another reason for her sabbatical: "I had to go away if I wanted to learn to be a human being."

On June 1980, the Patti Smith Group gave one final performance at the "Punch and Judy Theater Benefit Concert, Second Annual Detroit Symphony Benefit Concert." Joined by Fred, Kaye, Sohl, bassist Gary

Rasmussen, and the Stooges drummer Scott Asheton, the group performed several songs and included covers such as Bob. Dylan's "The Times They Are A-Changin,'" Cole Porter's "I Concentrate on You," and the Doors' "The End."

During this time, Smith was a stay-at-home mom. Nestled in an old stone home by a canal, Smith's creative output was minimal. Throughout the 1980s, Smith rarely performed, seemingly disappearing from the popular music scene and from those whom she had known before her new life. Although not performing music, Smith continued to write poetry and even performed readings as the opening act for the Fred's Sonic Rendezvous Band on October 9–10, 1981, at the Second Chance in Ann Arbor, Michigan.

For the early 1980s, Smith led a quiet life in Michigan. Clive Davis stayed in touch with her throughout the years, giving her the time to her family and not to her career. Davis later stated, "As the months of her hiatus extended into years, we would speak from time to time, every couple of years or so. I never asked for an album. She was immersed so deeply in her personal life that I just knew not to intrude on her privacy. She would record when she was ready."

Smith used this time as a matter of reflection and growth as well as to dedicate herself to her growing family, which included her son, Jackson, and, later, her daughter, Jesse. Motherhood began to have a profound effect on Smith, as she stated, "Now I really understand why my mother would cry if she saw an injured child on the news. When you have your own child, every other child becomes potentially yours." In addition to her responsibilities as a mother, Smith immersed herself in study, from the Bible to art history to Japanese literature.

A September 1986 mention in *Spin Magazine* marked a commercial announcement of Smith's comeback. Why after nine years would she suddenly have the desire to make a record? The genesis of the album began several years before its release. While Smith did not release any new music during her sabbatical, she continued to write material. In 1986, Smith began to rehearse and develop material with friends, and the kernel of the album began to take shape.

6

"I WAS LOOKING FOR YOU"

1986–1994

The musical and political climate that Smith was reintroducing herself into was quite different from the one that she left. Gone was the flower-power prime of the 1960s. Departed was the duality of danceable dissent with the 1970s. The 1980s were all about the individual. The channel Music Television, aka MTV, decried "I Want My MTV," and the world met the "my" with the most pronounced capital "M" that one could muster, ultimately leaving music cold and ready to be blindly ingested by the masses.

Independence of all kinds was on the minds of political leaders. The cold war saw the United States tightening diplomatic and economic pressures on the USSR, resulting in a frayed and divisive political climate. Tension filled the air, with the superpowers afraid of taking a step without the most dangerous of consequences. Meanwhile, Patti and Fred were simply happy with their self-imposed sabbatical in Michigan.

By mid-1986, Fred and Patti, along with Daugherty and Sohl, began to work on material for a new record. Titled *Dream of Life*, Patti enlisted the help of Jimmy Iovine, the impresario that gave life to her most commercially successful album, *Easter*. Although billed as a "Patti Smith" record, it's very much the "Patti and Fred" show, with the duo writing every song together. Patti spoke of their collaboration to Mary Anne Cassata for *The Music Paper*: "Working with Fred is very important to me. Our album represents us working together. We have a lot of other ideas and songs we haven't done yet. Many songs. We're looking into the future with some other works. We have achieved what we wanted with this album. What we wanted to do was a piece of work together that addressed the things we cared about."

As the material was developing, a clear theme was peeking its head through the material. Patti's lyrics leaned on the idea of communication and its importance in one's life, or as Smith stated, "the underlying principle is the communication between man and woman, between parent and child, between one and their creator. Planetary communication. It's positiveness behind hope, and also awareness of these kinds of difficult situations." This idea of communication permeated throughout the sessions as well with Smith noting that the personnel on the record worked well to achieve her and Fred's vision. Smith asserted, "It was a real collaboration on everyone's part. Everyone really did their part, from Richard Sohl to the assistant engineer. Everyone put so much into this production."

In her book *Patti Smith Complete: 1975–2006*, Smith also voiced that the power dynamic between herself and Fred created its own fair share of difficulties: "This was an extremely difficult album to create, with two highly self-critical people trying to please themselves as well as each other." Furthermore, Smith noted that Sohl acted as the impromptu referee at times, ultimately helping to serve the mission statement of the record: "We were aided by the patient and supportive Richard Sohl, who came to work with us for some months prior to recording. His sense of humor, his classical knowledge, and our long history enabled us to realize our efforts, bringing them out of exile into the world."

As *Dream of Life* was to be her big comeback record, it would be only fitting that Robert Mapplethorpe shoot the cover photo. The idea came from Fred, with Patti showing a little bit of apprehension, as it had been some time since the two soul mates saw each other, let alone spoken on the phone. It took everything in Patti to summon the courage that she needed to call Robert; however, right before she was about to make the call, her phone rang, and for a brief moment she felt that it might have been Robert on the other end. Instead, it was her friend Ina Meibach, who told Patti that Robert had been admitted to the hospital for AIDS-related pneumonia. Immediately stricken with anguish,

Smith clutched her stomach and began to cry, distraught that one of the first loves of her life would perish sooner than later.

It was now imperative that Patti speak to Robert, as his sudden bout with pneumonia showed the fragility of his condition. Feeling anxious about the prospect of speaking to Robert, Patti began to turn to minor chores to clear her mind. To summon the strength needed to call Robert, Patti decided to call Sam Wagstaff first. Wagstaff informed Patti that Robert was not doing well but that he himself was suffering from AIDS and was doing far worse. Stunned by this, Smith now knew that time was of the essence and that she had to speak to Robert immediately. Smith called Mapplethorpe, and although he sounded tired and weak, he immediately perked up by hearing the sound of her voice. The two made plans to meet in New York upon Robert's being healthy enough to have visitors.

Soon after, Smith and the family drove from Detroit to New York City to visit Robert. During her visit, Smith and Mapplethorpe paid their friend Sam a visit at St. Vincent's Hospital, where he was being kept in the AIDS ward, his body afflicted with sores. To soothe him, Patti began to sing a lullaby that she and Fred had written for their son, which would ultimately become "The Jackson Song," the closing song from *Dream of Life*.

A few weeks after, Smith and Mapplethorpe met up to take the album cover photo for *Dream of Life*. The photo was taken in Los Angeles, where Fred, Patti, and Iovine were working on recording material for *Dream of Life* and Mapplethorpe was visiting his youngest brother, Edward. While *Horses* signified the beginning of a movement, the cover of *Dream of Life* appears to signal the frailty of life. Clutching her left hand with her right, Smith seems worn and aged. Her black sweater makes her appear lost in the background of bushes, accented by the black-and-white portraiture. Her eyes appear deep yet sharp, as if she has found the dream of life but is not quite ready to share what the past nine years have taught her.

The aged look that I mention may very well have been pain or sadness. Mapplethorpe's body was rapidly deteriorating, and he was struggling to remain active and healthy. During the shoot, Mapplethorpe appeared frail and weak, but he marshaled through the shoot as best he could. Smith noted, "It was a simple photograph. My hair is braided like Frida Kahlo's. The sun is in my eyes. And I am looking at Robert and he is alive."

The album begins with the anthem "People Have the Power," a straightforward if not simplistic ode to people rising above and fighting for what they believe in. The idea for the song came from Fred, who one day interrupted Patti while she was washing dishes and said "People have the power. Write it." Fred and Patti wrote the song as a touchstone for people trying to express both individual and collective rights of power. The message of people doing their part to help their fellow men and women could have been easily sold in the post–Live Aid, 1980s America. The catalyst for the song came from her personal reflection about getting older and noticing how among all the pain in the world, humanity itself is a strong force. Smith stated, "Human beings are incredibly strong. The human race has survived world wars and plagues. If we're not all gifted with good situations in life, we are all gifted with personal strength. I refuse not to be optimistic."

The song's opening line, "I was dreaming in my dreaming," evokes the idea that the populous has been smacked by a political slumber, with Smith trying to shake the masses to "wrestle the world from fools." It's immediately apparent since the nine years from the release of *Wave* that Smith's delivery of such material is less to incite and more to report. Smith's delivery now appeared to be more akin to CNN reporting on Reagan-era atrocities than jumping into the crowd of disenchanted to fight the good fight. And with this song, Patti had successfully written an egalitarian canticle, complete with a robust chorus and sharp production value ready to explode over the masses. Smith proves that in an era rampant with hair metal, synth pop, and hip-hop, a good old-fashioned protest song could carry the substance of any top-40 hit.

"People Have the Power" was even given a music video treatment in an effort to sell Smith to the MTV generation. The video contains numerous music video tropes, including close-up shots of Smith writing the lyrics. "People Have the Power" was the lead single from *Dream of Life*, reaching number 19 on *Billboard Magazine*'s Mainstream Rock Charts and becoming a minor hit. Whereas the video or chart strength might have failed in attracting younger listeners or viewers, the song lived on as a populist anthem with presidential hopeful Ralph Nader using it as his campaign song during the 2000 presidential election. Additionally, Bruce Springsteen performed "People Have the Power" during "Vote for Change" campaign events throughout the 2004 election season.

The subsequent track, "Going Under," showcases Sohl's nimble yet gorgeous style. The mix allows Sohl's playing to appear to flow like a wave of water gently crashing on the ground, mirrored by the swooshing sound of the cymbals. Smith speaks of water being a metaphor for life or, as she's speaks toward the end of the song, "Shall we swim over and over? The curve of a wing, its destination ever changing." The line "its destination ever changing" is a beautiful and simplistic idea capturing one of the album's themes—life ebbing and flowing: that life will constantly change and, like the sea, its destination is ever changing.

The religious motif of water and rebirth appears throughout the lyrics to "Going Under." During a spoken-word portion of the song, Smith ponders, "Who will decide the shape of things, the shift of being?" warranting the thought of who or what will decide the form of humanity and its duration on this earth. When Smith sings, "The sea's foaming mane, it will serve us. We'll surface, and we'll plunge back again." The image of the "sea's foaming mane" could be seen as a reference to Poseidon, the Greek god of water. Specifically, Smith's inclusion of the line "foaming mane" juxtaposes the idea of foaming water with the mane of an animal. Artist Walter Crane depicts a similar picture with his 1893 painting *Neptune's Horses*, which at first glance shows a series of waves but upon closer inspection shows the waves to be a fleet of white horses crashing toward the shore.

The religious allegory continues with "Up There Down There," an up-tempo rock song that plays out like a musical sequel to the Rolling Stones' "Gimme Shelter," with Fred doing his best Keith Richards impersonation. Smith plays with abstraction by describing the sun as "some call it a spirit, some call it the sun" and that "its energies are not for hire, it serves man, it serves everyone." Smith places the sun in the role of serving all of humankind. Smith mirrors this idea of obedience by stating, "Down there where Jonah wails," which refers to the Biblical story of Jonah and the whale, one of the oddest accounts in the Bible, where God commands Jonah to preach repentance to the city of Nineveh. Jonah, not wanting to do such a command, boards a ship to Tarshish, where he is ultimately thrown overboard and into the mouth of a whale. Jonah, seeing the error of his ways, decides to pledge his obedience to God.

The question of what Smith is pledging allegiance to is raised with "Up There Down There." The song was recorded on February 22, 1987, on the day that Andy Warhol passed away. The most obvious answer is that Patti is pledging allegiance to Fred, or perhaps the allegiance being pledged is to all of humankind, which Smith comments on by stating, "It's all for man, it's for everyone, it's up there, down there." The arrangement of the song showcases Fred's guitar playing, which is a series of blues-inspired riffs accented by the somewhat mundane performance of the rhythm section. The result is an unfortunate misfire between Patti and Fred, whose dialogue between each other never quite fills the potential of the song.

Amid the tracking of the *Dream of Life*, Samuel Wagstaff passed away on January 14, 1987, at the age of sixty-five of pneumonia arising from AIDS-related complications. In a beautiful and stunning requiem, Patti penned the lyrics for "Paths That Cross," a lyrically straightforward tribute to her recently departed friend. The song is easily the most powerful song on the record with the theme of death not being final and that we all will eventually cross paths again, sentiments ringing both true and poignant.

Musically, the simple melody is supported by Fred's reverb-drenched acoustic guitar and Sohl's moving piano playing, allowing Smith's lyrics to take center stage. Smith perfectly balances emotional vulnerability and hushed remembrance with vocal flourishes that mute part of the lyric and quickly come back for the next word. Such an example is the line "a way I wish to know to know," where Smith gently mutes "wish" before coming back on "know."

Throughout "Paths That Cross," Patti never shows a hint of anger over having to say good-bye, but she is asking questions to further deal with the anguish that she is feeling. She laments, "Speak to me heart, I feel a needing to bridge the clouds" as a way of asking her heart to mend the feeling of sadness. Subsequently, she sings, "Speak to me heart, all things renew hearts will mend," ultimately deciding that in time her heart will rebuild itself. This simple idea of acknowledging pain and dealing with loss ends the first side of the album on an emotionally charged, however positive, note.

The album's title track is Patti at her most sentimental: the ultimate Hallmark card of approval for a life filled with love and ethereal bliss. The lyrics read like a letter to Fred or her family, with Patti gently delivering each line as if every syllable is as delicate as the love in her life is. The song more than suggests the happiness that Smith's sabbatical from performing has warranted her. Smith captures this with the line "deep in my heart, how the presence of you shines, in a light to last a whole life through," positing that the love that she has in her heart is all that is needed to sustain her life. With "Dream of Life," Patti foresees an optimistic future and doesn't appear to really care about anything else other than the love she feels. Smith sings, "I recall the wonder of it all, each dream of life I'll share with you," hypothesizing that each day for her is a gift and she cannot wait to carry out her days with such bliss.

Whereas the political mindfulness of the album opened with "People Have the Power," the song "Where Duty Calls" amplifies this sentiment with real-world consequence. The song is written in memory of the victims of the Beirut Barracks Bombings, an event that occurred on October 23, 1983, during the Lebanese Civil War where two trucks filled with bombs collided with two separate buildings, killing 299 American and French servicemen—servicemen who were there to lend their support to the Lebanese government and its people.

On an album that celebrates a new life filled with love, the song is striking in its thematic approach to the other songs on the album. Musically and lyrically, the song begins with the same idea of what the victims might have felt at the time, with them quietly sleeping in their beds before the attack. Fred plays a light guitar motif that feels dreamlike while a wind instrument plays in the background. Patti reinforces this tranquil picture by setting the scene with the lyrics "In a room in Lebanon, they silently slept. They were dreaming crazy dreams in a foreign alphabet."

Smith and the group reflect the violence of the day by rapidly adding crescendos and increasing the tempos dramatically. By shifting the articulations of the music, the group adds drama and conflict to reflect the mind-set of the nation and those who perished that day. The bridge of the song features a spoken-word passage where Smith speaks about communication by enlisting the way that the sun and the moon communicate with each other: "the sun blooms awake into the glare of all our little wars. Who pray to return the salute the coming and dying of the moon." This idea of the sun and moon saluting each other evokes the cyclical nature of communication and how goals are met and accomplishments are seen with proper communication.

Smith ends the song with an ode to the Bible verse Luke 23:34, which originally stated, "Father, forgive them, for they know not what they do. And they parted his raiment, and cast lots." In her version, Smith asks God to forgive the bombers by singing, "Forgive them Father they know not what they do. From the vast portals of their consciousness, they're calling to you." Smith is surmising that the bombers on that day were ultimately looking for salvation and a higher calling: that deep down inside their acts, though evil in their execution, they were trying to help them seek a higher power.

"Looking for You (I Was)" is a simple, subtle song that best exemplifies the more pop-oriented sound that *Dream of Life* produced. While the more polished sound that Iovine helped to create was very much of the time, "Looking for You (I Was)" contains a lot of the 1980s flourishes that were brandished on popular music at the time. Musically, the song can be seen as a kissing cousin to Bryan Adams's 1984 hit "Summer of '69," with both songs beginning with a simple hit on the snare drum, followed by a guitar riffing on a major chord. The call and response of Smith singing the main hook "looking for you" with her voice responding with "looking for you" feels as if the song could have been recorded by a female rock group of the era, such as the Bangles or the Go-Go's.

Smith playfully casts a scene that takes the listener toward two descriptions of love, which she sings to her suitor: one description being in metaphor and one in contemporary tongue. Smith sets the stage by describing a "medieval night" where love is in the air and the sky is so porous that "wishes fall" and she yearns to "wish on them all." Smith describes that she yearns to be her suitor's "destiny," but ultimately it's her very heart that "obscured the view."

Later in the song, Smith returns to the same sentiment but with a modern flair by stating, "All that heart's desire was written before us in the medieval fire, it was love's design." With the previous stanza, Smith harkens back to the first stanza by stating, "All that heart's desire was written before us," deducing that the stars foretold their love before they even knew. At the end of the song, Smith includes a brief spoken-word passage where she offers the terrain in which she was "looking" by speaking, "From the Portobello Road to the Port of Marseilles," giving the romantic notion of two European lovers looking for each other in the undercurrent of the stars.

Smith concludes *Dream of Life* with "The Jackson Song," a tender lullaby to her son. Utilizing only voice, piano, harp, and cello, the song has an ethereal quality that pleasantly lulls the listener into a soft slumber. Sohl backs this quality by repeating a Bb chord within a waltz, following the rhythm of a rocking chair and providing a rhythmic pulse for the song. As with traditional lullabies, the lyrics offer advice or life lessons to the recipient of the lullaby. Smith offers such advice as "May your path be your own, but I'm with you. And each day you'll go," ostensibly telling Jackson that as you journey through life, you'll never be without your mother. The song was difficult for Smith, as it brought out a lot of her emotions that ultimately shaped her performance. Smith stated, "What happened was that I missed my cue at the end. I came in a little too late because I got real moved to enter the song again. After hearing the song we decided it was all right and left it that way."

As much as the song can be viewed as a lullaby to Jackson, the song could be seen as a swan song to Mapplethorpe. Mapplethorpe visited the group while it recorded "The Jackson Song." Incredibly ill and weak during his visit, he lay down in the control room while the band recorded. Before recording, Fred turned to Richard and gave him the instruction "Make them cry." After performing the song twice, Patti looked into the control and saw Mapplethorpe asleep while Fred stood above him weeping. A gentle gesture that capped off *Dream of Life*.

Davis was impressed with *Dream of Life* and was happy to see Smith back in the musical saddle. Upon its release, Davis stated, "As soon as I started playing it, I felt as though we'd picked up without missing a beat. The urgency was still there. Maybe with more maturity, more reflection, but with the same impact." Davis was also quick to point out the songs "Paths That Cross" and "Up There Down There" as adding "beauty and drama" to *Dream of Life*.

The critical community opened its arms to Patti and welcomed her back to the fold. Several were quick to point out that her nine-year absence served only to strengthen her sound and mature her voice. In his review in *Rolling Stone*, critic Robert Palmer stated, "The thought and care that evidently went into the creation of this album should be a lesson to certain rock icons who have been churning out dreary product on schedule, rather than taking the time to create a music, and a vision, worthy of their talents."

In his review in *Penthouse*, critic Vin Scelsa stated that the album had sweet, wonderful writing: "strong, moving images set to often quite beautiful accompaniment." Scelsa stated, "The tracks are full of musical touchstones (the Native American rhythm of 'Going Under,' the 'na na na na' riff in the title song); the melodies are memorable; and the band, including former mates Jay Dee Daugherty and Richard Sohl, is strong and in sync with Patti's vision."

Scelsa's comments regarding Smith's "former mates" Daugherty and Sohl perfectly encapsulate the overall tone of the record. Whatever history Smith, Daugherty, and Sohl cultivated before the recording seems to be lost in the mix. That ensemble interplay that made the Patti Smith Group so raw isn't apparent on the record, resulting in a some-what false sound. Such a thought did not occur to Smith, instead voic-ing, "I'm happy with the whole album. I love it all. All the work I've done in the past is important to me. Anything I've ever done, I've put a lot of care into. People will have to decide for themselves what they feel about the album. This is an album that cannot be defined."

This false sound could have been the production value of the time or perhaps Smith's more sentimental side rearing its head on the record. Jon Pareles of the *New York Times* mentions this in his review by stating, "Ms. Smith's sentimental streak, once balanced by her wild-eyed intensity, has grown overwhelming during her sabbatical. Song after song brings up dreams, paradise, the sea and the sky, with hardly any grit to offset them."

With a slew of positive reviews ahead of her, Smith appeared poised to make a bona fide comeback. However, she was not able to mirror her success in the 1970s. Part of the reason was Patti's lack of touring in support of the record, partly because she gave birth to her daughter, Jesse. Knowing all too well the affect that the road can have on a person, Smith decided not to tour, stating, "I don't think that touring and children mix. The road is not a healthy place for a child to be."

Smith's return to the music scene after her sabbatical could repre-sent an overall feeling about the music of the 1970s in general. In addition to *Dream of Life*, other releases from artists of the 1960s and 1970s suffered similar fates. Boz Scagg's *Other Roads*, Brian Wilson's *Brian Wilson*, and Jimmy Page's *Outrider* all failed to make an impression in sales. The public's reaction to the record didn't appear to faze Smith at all. Smith spoke of this by saying, "Once you record, mix it and whatever, it no longer belongs to you. It goes out to the world. The idea here is to do a good piece of work. I say, do something you think the people will like." In a 1996 interview in *Q Magazine*, Smith provided another reason for the poor reception to *Dream of Life*: "When we recorded *Dream of Life*, it was not entirely artistic. I was having my second child and it becomes expensive. But my heart wasn't really in a full comeback anyway and the album got no airtime in America."

After the *Dream of Life* episode concluded, Smith and the family headed back to Michigan to continue their self-imposed sabbatical. What was to be their return to happiness both personally and professionally ultimately became a time of great sorrow. The resulting turmoil that Patti experienced would take her away from the spotlight and mold the next creative phase in her career.

Smith's string of sorrow began on March 9, 1989, when Mapplethorpe passed away from complications stemming from his fight with AIDS. His death did not come as a surprise to Patti, mainly because she had spoken to him the night before and knew in her heart that his death was near. Smith received the phone call that he had passed while watching a presentation of the Puccini opera *Tosca* on A&E. Perhaps out of shock or genuine happiness, Smith's immediate reaction was of excitement, as she knew that his suffering was over and his new adventure to the afterlife had begun. On May 22, 1989, Patti and Fred drove to New York to attend a service held at the Whitney Museum. In tribute to Robert, Patti sang a song that she had written expressing the importance of saying good-bye. Unfortunately, Patti would have to say good-bye many times.

Mapplethorpe's passing was not only a loss but also the closing of a door in Smith's life. From her introduction to the New York art community, Mapplethorpe had been her lover, partner, and confidant. Although not actively recording or performing during this time, Smith did not let her creative juices remain stagnant. On March 17, 1990, Smith and Sonic performed "People Have the Power" and Bob Dylan's "A Hard Rain's A-Gonna Fall" at New York's Radio City Music Hall as a part of an evening titled "That's What Friends Are For: Arista Records 15th Anniversary Concert." The concert featured a who's who of Arista Records' staple of artists, including Whitney Houston, Barry Manilow, and Hall and Oates, with the sales going directly to the Gay Men's Health Crisis and other AIDS organizations. Not two months later, Richard Sohl would succumb to a heart attack at the age of thirty-seven.

In the spring of 1991, Smith began working on what would become *Woolgathering*, a collection of vignettes, poems, and memoir about her childhood. Reviewing the reissue released in 2011, David L. Ulin of the *Los Angeles Times* perfectly captures the book's aesthetics as well as the juxtapositions found in her work by stating, "There it is, that mix of the practical and the mythic, like the marriage of rock 'n' roll and poetry." In 1993, Smith would briefly return to the concert stage as part of Central Park's "Summer Stage" concert series. She told Evelyn McDonnell of the *Village Voice* that the concert was "one of the happiest nights of my life. I couldn't believe how great these people were. The whole atmosphere—not just the audience, but I had my brother there, and Fred was there, and so I have really happy memories of it."

By the early 1990s, "Sonic" Smith's health began to be questioned by his former band mates in the Sonic Rendezvous Band. After a show, Gary Rasmussen stated, "It wasn't 'til when [MC5 front man] Rob Tyner died, we did a benefit and I think Fred was just . . . it was starting to show then, really, that something might be wrong with Fred. He was lookin' kinda funny, maybe his life just caught up with him. I talked to Patti, and Patti and Fred would be goin', 'Oh, Fred has these allergies now.' I never wanted to push him on it. I just said, 'Oh, well that's too bad. Maybe it's just a little thing he's going through and he'll be better.'"

On November 4, 1994, Patti was dealt a most devastating blow when Fred passed away at the tender age of forty-five. A few days before his passing, Fred collapsed at home and was admitted to St. John's Hospital, ultimately succumbing to heart failure.

At the time of his death, he was working on a compilation of Sonic's Rendezvous live material and writing songs for an upcoming album with Patti. Lenny Kaye mentioned at the time of his passing, "He was teaching her guitar. That was always one of her dreams, to learn how to play guitar. She showed me all her chords, and she plays them pretty well." After Fred's passing, Patti took solace in song, often listening to Dylan's *World Gone Wrong* and Nirvana's *Unplugged*, hoping that art could help mend her broken heart.

"When I lost my husband, I felt completely desolate," she said. "From him I learned a more compassionate view of the general populace. He was much more compassionate about those who will inherit the earth than I. But after he died, I did the best work I have done in fifteen years. The quality of my singing has strengthened. That's my legacy from my husband."

As if losing three of the closest men in her life over a five-year period wasn't hard enough, Patti's brother Todd passed away on December 4, 1994. The last time Patti saw Todd was the Thanksgiving of that year, shortly after Fred passed away. Always her rock, Todd took her for a drive and played the soundtrack to the movie *Natural Born Killers*, which featured her song "Rock and Roll Nigger." Todd offered his kind words of support by saying, "You're gonna make it, and I'll be there. You'll do new work and take it to the people and I'll be right by your side."

With sorrow surrounding her, Patti began to mourn the only way that she knew how . . . through her art.

7

"WITH A STRANGE WAY OF WALKING AND A STRANGE WAY OF BREATHING"

1994–1996

While the record industry into which Patti reintroduced herself upon the release of *Dream of Life* in 1988 may not have been the most supportive of acts of her generation, the record-buying public of the mid-1990s appeared prime for a Patti Smith resurgence. The record industry was in a postgrunge haze, with the unfortunate suicide of Nirvana front man Kurt Cobain appearing to be the death rattle of the entire grunge scene.

Teenagers at this time had proven that they were interested in punk rock textures, with the band the Offspring selling more than twenty million copies of its third studio album, *Smash*, and with Green Day selling more than twenty million albums of its third studio album, *Dookie*, the latter featuring an illustrated picture of Smith's third album, *Easter*, in the lower right-hand corner in a "Where's Waldo?"–esque collage.

Strong-selling female-fronted acts and solo artists were at an all-time high, with recent releases by the Fugees, Tori Amos, and Joan Osborne burning the record charts and moving impressive amounts of units. Additionally, older established punk rock bands and CBGB-affiliated acts were still on the radar of the American public, with the Sex Pistols announcing a reunion tour, the Ramones going on a farewell tour, and a David Byrne–less Talking Heads releasing the cleverly titled album, *No*

Talking, Just Head. It would appear that 1996 would be a good a time as any for Patti Smith to make her official comeback.

The germination of her comeback began in 1995 with Patti slowly returning to active performing. On New Year's Day, Patti did a reading of "People Have the Power" and a rendition of "Ghost Dance" with Lenny Kaye at the Poetry Project at St. Mark's Church in New York. The next month, Smith accepted an invitation from Allen Ginsberg to perform before a sold-out crowd of four thousand at Hill Auditorium in Ann Arbor. After a smattering of appearances in Michigan throughout the year, Smith performed a full evening of material on July 5, 1995, at the Phoenix Club in Toronto. Evelyn McDonnell of *The Village Voice* was there for the event, and by her account, Smith did not disappoint. McDonnell asserted, "The woman who brought a shamanistic force to punk's tattered style is in an expressive trance. She seems unconscious of her elegant, long-boned fingers as they flutter before her, or as she crosses her arms over her chest and rests her hand on her shoulders, anchoring body to earth."

In December 1995, Patti received the boost that she needed to officially bring her back to active performing. Bob Dylan asked her to be his opening act for the East Coast leg of his "Paradise Lost" tour. Assembling a band that consisted of Kaye, Daugherty, Verlaine, bassist Tony Shanahan, and guitarist Oliver Ray, Smith referred to this time as having a positive influence on her life and helping to shake off the "performance dust." A memorable part of the tour was when Patti sang the song "Dark Eyes" with Dylan on several dates.

Joining them on tour was REM front man Michael Stipe, who became the tour's de facto photographer. Patti first spoke to Michael on Valentine's Day 1995 while Michael was in Barcelona. Michael called to wish her a happy Valentine's Day, knowing that being without Fred on the day would be hard for her. In Stipe's book *Two Times Intro: On the Road with Patti Smith*, Patti would look back on that day and say about Stipe, "That was the first time we spoke, and the last time he would be a stranger."

Smith began 1996 by getting the opportunity to induct the Velvet Underground into the Rock and Roll Hall of Fame at the Waldorf Astoria in New York. Smith inducted the band the only way that she knew how—with a free-form prose mirroring the "everything plus the kitchen sink" aural blast that the band exuded. Patti mentions, "They were a band of opposites, shooting pole to pole, without apology, with dissonant beauty. Trampling the flowers of peacemakers. Treading the blind depths." As much as Patti uses these words to abstractly describe the Velvet Underground, she unknowingly describes the next phase in her career: an unapologetic period of mourning, exploring paradoxes, challenging all notions . . . and doing so with righteousness.

Smith and Co. began to culminate material for a new album, resulting in the album *Gone Again*. To assist in bringing the collection of songs to life, Smith and Co. enlisted the help of Canadian musician/producer Malcolm Burn, whose discography consisted of production duties on albums by the Neville Brothers, Iggy Pop, and John Mellencamp, to name a few. Bringing this second phase of her career full circle, Smith recorded the album at Electric Lady Studios in New York, where her aural journey had begun.

To fill the void left by Sohl, Smith turned to Detroit-based pianist/keyboardist Luis Resto. Resto's résumé up to this point included stints in the band Was (Not Was) as well as record dates with jazz saxophonist Dave McMurray and R&B artists Anita Baker and Wendy Moten. Subsequent to his work with Smith, Resto would win an Academy Award and a Grammy Award for his work with rapper Eminem for the 2002 movie *8 Mile*. Resto began playing the piano at the age of nine, receiving his initial inspiration to pursue music from his grandmother, herself a pianist. While working with Don Was in Los Angeles, Resto received a phone call from a friend asking him how his life in Los Angeles was going. Resto was slowly building a career for himself on the West Coast, becoming a session musician for hire. The friend asked if Resto would be interested in working with Patti, although Resto was initially confused, as he did not know if his friend was referring to Smith or Patti Smyth, the lead singer of the 1980s rock band Scandal.

Resto, like his entire generation, was introduced to Smith via *Horses*. "When I saw her *Horses* album, she just knocked me out at the time. When she starts with 'Jesus died for someone's sins, but not mine' I was thirteen and I was like 'wow' and she just rocked." Not really interested in staying in Los Angeles, Resto journeyed back east to work on the *Gone Again* sessions. Resto states that the sessions for the record "were awesome" and recording with Patti "continues to be one of the highpoints of my career because of her humanity, artistry and her being."

Gone Again is an album of dualities: life and death, acoustic and electric, a play on the fastballs that life can throw. Smith was out to prove that despite the rough couple of years that she experienced, the passing of the men in her life did not have to be expressed in macabre circumstances. Smith spoke about the album being therapeutic: that it gave her a forum where she could express her grief while reminding everyone that even amid great difficulty or sadness, one should be grateful and optimistic.

Arista Records was banking on Smith's return and the release of *Gone Again* as being the rebirth of the female rock-and-roll star, which was fitting at this time, as Smith could clearly be seen as an influence to the next generation of female rock stars. Arista's executive vice president and general manager Roy Lott was quick to point out with the release of *Dream of Life* that the record company did not understand the weight of her influence but, over time, had come to appreciate her and an entire generation built on her music. Lott further stated, "Today, [many] major artists are fans of Patti Smith, their music is colored by Patti Smith, so her music is more in tune with what the consumers have been buying."

Enough time had passed for the contemporary rock scene to officially list Smith as an influence. The mid-1990s rock-and-roll scene had produced a fair share of female rock stars who found a clear influence in Smith. While periodicals were quick to find Smith's influence in the work of singer/songwriter PJ Harvey and Hole front woman Courtney Love, many failed to find the influence of Smith among those in her generation. Cleveland-based singer/songwriter Adele Bertei was performing at blues bars in the 1970s and saw Smith as not only an influence but a teacher of sorts. Bertei asserts, "At the time music was about divas or rock goddesses. It was nothing to do with boyish little tykes like myself who could sing blues. I didn't think there'd ever be a place for me. Then Patti Smith came out with an album that rocked my universe. She was androgynous, outspoken, obviously well-educated and well-read. She became like a mentor to me. If she dropped references to Brancusi [the Romanian sculptor], I'd go out and find art books. If it was Rimbaud, I'd read him and learn about the French decadents. Because I didn't have much of an education, Smith in a sense was my first teacher."

Arista's marketing team saw an opportunity to sell Smith to the entire postgrunge, mid-1990s rock-and-roll scene. In congruence with the release of Smith's book *The Coral Sea*, the book's publisher W. W. Norton began handing out bookmarks advertising the new album at Smith's book signings and readings. Additionally, Arista sold a remastered box set of her first four albums, which included live material as well as material that did not make the original records, clearly indicating that Arista was ready to not only reintroduce Smith to her original fans but introduce her to an entirely new generation of listeners who were not even alive when she had her initial success.

The album cover reflects the passing of time, with gradients that appear both sepia and standard black and white. Taken by Annie Leibovitz, the cover photo features Smith as a sullen, contemplative woman who has amassed several years under her belt. With her head down, Smith has a leather jacket over her left shoulder with her hand to her mouth, perhaps as a sign that she is trying to hide the words coming out of her mouth. The cover plays in direct opposition to that of her first album. *Horses* features Smith with a cocksure attitude and a jacket over her left shoulder, while *Gone Again* features the same position, although Smith's sullen appearance plays as if life has worn her down. Perhaps a gesture to the passing of time, Smith's jacket on the *Gone Again* cover is a leather jacket, showing that the one that she had on the cover of *Horses* has aged.

The atmosphere of the album's first track, "Gone Again," at times feels as if it's taking place during a tribal or religious ceremony. This feeling is most indicative of the Native American practice known as a "ghost dance," which is the practice of a dance that would reconcile the living with the souls of those who have departed and, if successful, bring unity and prosperity to all. This idea of the album's title track being a tribal song is fitting, as Smith had experienced so much loss and may have wanted to reunite with her loved ones through such a dance.

The song's Native American spirit and tone were due to Fred, whose heritage included Native American ancestry. Fred wanted Patti to lyrically capture the storytelling qualities that would occur in tribes. Patti sings of having a "winter's tail" and briefly tells a story of "vagrant hearts" and how they "seize the sky and they're gone again." Patti could very well be talking about Fred as a "vagrant heart," as having sowed his "seed into the wind," which could be Patti's way of thanking him for having been a part of her life.

In conversation with *Rolling Stone*'s David Fricke, Smith stated that the song was meant to be one of renewal, that she was to be the woman of the tribe who speaks about the history of the tribe: their struggles, their downfalls, and the warriors that gave their lives to support them. Musically, the drummers are ultimately what capture the Native American aspect of the song by performing simple passages on the toms, painting a picture of a tribe festooned in native regalia dancing and trying to speak to those who have departed. This may also be supported by Smith's vocal embellishments on this song, with her slurred "na-na-na's" invoking a transcendent quality to the piece. What is most exciting about the album's title track is that it shows Smith venting her anger regarding the loss that she has experienced in her life. When Smith ends each verse with "gone again," it's sung not with sadness but anger. Smith digs deep within her herself and lets out aggression when singing the lyric, as if to let the grief out to let the love in.

This idea of transcendence bleeds into the subsequent song, "Beneath the Southern Cross," a melancholy ballad that features only voice, acoustic guitar, and electric guitar. Smith performs a majority of the song a D major chord that drones throughout, allowing a basic musical framework for her vocals to take center stage. Lyrically, Smith is speaking about shedding the mortal coil and leaving one's physical body. Smith's stating "gone, this maze of being skin" reflects this idea of no longer being in one's body and having left to venture to a different plain outside the "maze" of existence.

Smith is most likely referring to Heaven, with "cross over" being an indication, but in the same token, she mentions, "Anyone gone to greet lame, the inspired sky," which could refer to the constellation "Southern Cross." To the aboriginal people of Australia, the Southern Cross was called Mirrabooka, a kind and clever man immortalized by being put into the night sky by Biami, the creator. This was to assist with watching over the people on Earth. Smith may be stating that the "cross over" is not necessarily Heaven but becoming a star or constellation to look over those still of this Earth.

"Beneath the Southern Cross" is given an additional breath of heavenly character with the inclusion of singer-songwriter Jeff Buckley's vocal line toward the end, which has a stringlike quality, as if his vocal line was being bowed by a violin, as opposed to being sung by a voice. This added embellishment by Buckley provides a gentle end to the song, made all the more eerie as it was Buckley's last studio date before his untimely death on May 29, 1997, at the all too young age of thirty.

The scent of death continued to linger throughout the album with the song "About a Boy," serving as a letter of grief and anger. The song is about and in memory of Kurt Cobain, who on April 5, 1994, took his own life at the age of twenty-seven. Cobain's struggle with heroin and fame became his ultimate undoing and served to strip a generation of its idol. The day that Cobain took his life, Fred and Patti visited a record store and saw kids outside it crying. Fighting the urge to comfort them, Smith decided to remain silent, deciding to channel her urge to comfort through song.

Smith was vocal about her heartbreak as well as her anger upon learning of Cobain's death. Smith had felt a maternal failure. In a 2012 interview with *Seattle News Weekly*, she stated, "I was heartbroken when he committed suicide. I loved Nirvana." She added, "We felt so badly. We just wished we would have known him, and been able to talk to him, and had some positive effect on him." Smith spoke of Cobain by stating her anger was attributed to seeing Mapplethorpe struggle to keep his life while Cobain was all too eager to end his. Smith said, "When you watch someone you care for fight so hard to hold their life, then see another person just throw their life away, I guess I had less patience for that."

With "About a Boy," Smith easily shifts the tone from a grieving, heartbroken mother to an angry fan. After an introduction laced with guitar feedback and auxiliary noise, Smith softly sings, "Toward another he has gone to breathe an air beyond his own," invoking the sense that Smith is saying good-bye to yet another person as he makes his way to the afterlife. However, with the lyric "from a chaos raging sweet," Smith changes her tone to reflect more anger, as if to say that she is tired of saying good-bye, tired of losing yet another person, especially within the circumstances that the world lost Cobain.

The song's title is a play on the Nirvana song "About a Girl," which first appeared on the band's 1989 album *Bleach*. The chorus of "about a boy, beyond it all" contains a duality that Smith was looking to express. On one hand, Smith is expressing that those who are "beyond it all" are those who are beyond responsibility, beyond mortal expressions of consequence. On the other, the phrase can mean beyond all earthly things and, hopefully, beyond all earthly pain that an individual could experience during one's life.

From *Horses* until *Gone Again*, Smith's voice and vocal capabilities continued to improve and mature. With each album, Smith developed a specific sound that at times appeared harsh and abrasive and at others was sweet and beautiful. Smith had developed a sonic vocabulary where she could easily express emotions by altering her voice to suit the lyric at hand. This is apparent in the song "My Madrigal," which is quite possibly the most beautifully sung performance on any of her records.

"My Madrigal" refers to the "madrigal" song form, a type of secular musical device that aims to convey the emotion of each syllable in a poetic fashion. "My Madrigal" plays more like an aria than a madrigal, with the entirety of *Gone Again* appearing to be Patti's opera about love and loss. Cowritten with Resto, the song begins with Resto playing a jazz-infused chord melody that quickly turns into a melancholy progression. Smith gently sings, "We waltzed beneath motionless skies," with Resto mirroring the waltz feel of the piece with airy flourishes.

Smith's delivery of the line "We expressed such sweet vows" is so filled with emotion that the listener expects her to instantly begin crying, as if the dialogue that she is trying to express is too much to bear. Smith returns to the line "We waltzed beneath motionless skies" later in the song, but the sudden key change adds additional weight to the words, as if the phrase bears repeating so that its recipient can understand its weight. With this song, one can't help but feel that Smith is musically saying good-bye to Fred and that life must go on. Smith's ending the song with "Till death do us part" displays the validity of the vows that she took with Fred and how she must move forward with her life.

A direct antithesis to her performance on "My Madrigal" can be found on the album's single "Summer Cannibals," an upbeat track with Smith delivering an aggressive, almost absurd performance. A major theme of the song is the notion that temptation can ultimately consume you, especially if you turn your back to it. Lyrically, Smith speaks about the temptation of the flesh. Smith sings, "The flesh was lean and the women moved forward like piranhas in a stream," painting a picture that temptation is pure to consume.

Ultimately, the character in the story decides not to partake by sing-ing, "And it all got too damn much for me," before offering herself as "another piece of meat" for the animals to enjoy. The lack of hesitation that Patti sings about signifies that she is ready to be adored again, that she is ready to give herself back to her fans as a unit of sustenance. This idea of sacrifice carries a fair amount of weight. The lyric "They circled around me natives in the ring" closely resembles "The Sacrifice" move-ment from composer Igor Stravinsky's *The Rite of Spring*. In this move-ment, after various primitive rituals celebrating the advent of spring, a young girl is chosen as a sacrificial victim and dances herself to death. Taking the simile that Smith provides of comparing women to piranha, the "circling" that the natives display in "Summer Cannibals" is the circling that young women engage in Stravinsky's seminal work.

A strong Dylan influence is felt on the track "Dead to the World," a mellow country song where Smith employs Dylan-esque vocal twangs and articulations. Using a waltz, Smith flips the usual "woman gone done me wrong" style of country music on its head by telling a story of how she fell under the influence of love and how it changed her way of life. The lyric "I formed me a presence whose aspect was changing" denotes how Smith was looking to make a change in her life. One could assume what Patti is referring to is Fred coming into her life at a junction in her career where she was beginning to make important decisions about her life and where she saw her future.

Along with the theme of when Fred and Patti met, the lyrics paint a picture of their first time together and how it may not have ended in Patti's favor. The lyric "I opened my coat but he never came closer, I bolted the door and I whispered oh well" makes it seem as if Patti made an advance to Fred and was shot down: a surprisingly explicit yet heart-warming lyric when considered in retrospect.

The country influence bleeds into the track "Wing," which one could see as the artistic cousin of "Dead to the World," with its waltz feel and tale of love and woe. From the get-go, the song harkens to a simpler time when love didn't complicate the implicit freedom of life. Smith sings, "And I was free, needed nobody and it was beautiful," observing that her blissful lack of having to answer to anyone—romantically, pro-fessionally, or otherwise—was the ultimate period of freedom.

In addition to this, Smith notices how not being on anyone's radar or living up to anyone's expectation could result in a free and beautiful life.

By singing, "I was a vision in another eye and they saw nothing, no future at all yet I was free," Smith is debating that a lack of expectation from those who expect you to produce something could itself be a form of happiness. The "other eye" in question could be a parent, or perhaps it could have been Arista Records after her subsequent sabbatical.

Smith continues the acoustic reflection with "Ravens," a Celtic-infused waltz that expands the harmonic palette of the record by incorporating both the accordion and the mandolin. Taking the Celtic-themed feel of the song, the symbol of the raven can be seen as both a positive attribute and a negative one. On the positive side, "to have a raven's knowledge" is an Irish proverb meaning to be particularly wise and prophetic. Ravens were the favorite bird of the god Lugh, the Celtic god of artists and artisans.

On the negative side, ravens were linked to darkness and death—especially the death of warriors in battle. Celtic war goddesses often took the form of a raven. In the Middle Welsh tale "The Dream of Rhonabwy," the knight Owein battles King Arthur with the assistance of ravens. Smith chooses to use the raven as a bearer of future events and, ultimately, to represent what we will become after we perish. Smith voices the idea of the raven being used as foreshadowing of our deaths with the line "before our feet a feather drifts," as if to say death is not far off. Additionally, the raven is used as a representation of the afterlife, which Smith explains by singing, "'Cause time will bid and make us rise, make ravens of us all." Smith explains through these passages that our lives, at some point, will cease and we will become ravens and fly into the afterlife.

Smith ends the acoustic trifecta of "Dead to the World," "Wing," and "Ravens" with a cover of Dylan's "Wicked Messenger." The song first appeared on Dylan's 1967 album *John Wesley Harding*, his first album to be released after three albums of electric guitar–infused rock and roll. Whereas Dylan's version is an acoustic-driven romp, Smith's is a stripped-down, no-holds-barred rock song complete with distortion, feedback, and rich articulations.

Lyrically, Dylan derives the title from Proverbs 13:17: "A wicked messenger falleth into mischief: but a faithful ambassador is health." In the song, the character first appears in public, unbidden, as an obsessive. The wicked messenger is the artist, the prophet, the protest singer. Smith, being an obvious Dylan fan, appears to be aligning herself with

Dylan by including this song on the record. Furthermore, Smith may be making a late declaration or commitment to music by making the musical statement that she is here, she is back, and she is bringing the good word.

"Fireflies" provides *Gone Again* with its most atmospheric and at times menacing sonic colors. Smith and Co. craft an alarming sound by primarily using minor chords, sparse percussion, and vocal inflections, made all the more challenging with its running time of 9 minutes 33 seconds. Smith begins the song with uneasy moans while Jeff Buckley returns, performing whirling-like sounds on an Egyptian string instrument called an "essrange," providing an otherworldly undertone to the track.

Patti uses the lyrics as a means of portraying the link between life and death and the journey that one takes to get there. By singing, "The ghost of thy ghost, walk I will walk," Smith is depicting herself as a ghost slowly journeying toward the afterlife. Smith expresses this by repeating the line "Eleven steps till I can rest, eleven steps till I'm blessed by you," counting down to nine, seven, until the music slowly and effortlessly fades away.

However sad or melancholy *Gone Again* appears, Smith ends the album on a positive note with "Farewell Reel," an acoustic track that perfectly concludes the arc of the record. Smith invites the listener into the song by stating what the chords of the song are, almost waving the listeners to grab their guitars and play along. Smith eschews most metaphorical devices in an attempt to clearly deliver a message to Fred. Smith makes peace with Fred by singing, "So darling farewell, all will be well," assuring him that everyone and everything will be okay. Smith reconciles the idea that however bad something might be ("But when it rains, it rains on me"), the journey and ultimate outcome will be beautiful ("And a rainbow appears life a smile from heaven").

If *Dream of Life* failed to be Smith's comeback, then *Gone Again* was the resurrection that no one saw coming. Among those who were most excited was Clive Davis, who stated in an article in *Billboard Magazine*, "I haven't really looked forward to an album as much as I have *Gone Again*." Davis further stated, "To have her come back with this album is wonderful. There's nothing out there that will touch people as much as this one will."

Among the postgrunge haze, Smith was a warm welcome back to the modern rock-and-roll scene. Critics welcomed Smith back with open arms and were quick to sing her praises. Scott Isler from *Newsday* mentions, "*Gone Again* is a triumph—not just for the return of Patti Smith, but on behalf of those she commemorates." In praising *Gone Again* for its strength, David Fricke of *Rolling Stone* mentions toward the end of his review, "It has been way too long between records and tours for her, but her sense of timing and strength of commitment have not failed her," alluding to the idea that the modern music scene was ripe for her return.

Critics and the general public were quick to point out how Patti's string of losses was unfortunate but nonetheless helped to elevate the material to new heights. David Browne in *Entertainment Weekly* echoes this sentiment by stating, "As insensitive as it might be to say, the succession of tragedies has lent a much-needed focus (and terseness) to Smith's work. Death becomes her—and not merely in her lyrics." Although Browne ultimately gave the album a grade of A–, he stated, "What Gone Again lacks is voltage. On only a few of the 11 songs does she charge ahead like the Smith of old, although when she does—as with the warpath cry of the title track—the ground shakes." The album proved to be a successful venture, ultimately reaching 55 on *Billboard Magazine*'s Top 200. Additionally, the album was named one of the top albums of 1996 by several periodicals, including the *Village Voice*, *Eye Weekly Canadian Critics Poll*, and *Mojo*.

Before the release of *Gone Again*, Arista worked hard on promoting Patti and getting the album into the hands of fans both old and new. On May 18, 1996, Patti and the band taped an appearance on the late-night program *Saturday Night Special*, with comedienne Roseanne Barr introducing the band by stating, "It's an honor for me to be able to introduce our next guest who's a legend and my idol, Patti Smith," perhaps showing how far-reaching Patti's influence truly was. The next month, Patti performed on *Late Night with David Letterman*, where Letterman introduced her by calling her "the legendary Patti Smith." A week after *Gone Again* was released in North America, Smith and the band played two sold-out dates at Irving Plaza in New York City to a welcoming hometown crowd. In his review for the *New York Times*, critic Neil Strauss voiced how the popular music community would have more of her in the future. Strauss stated, "Her tone, a combination of motherly advice and youthful anger, showed she still has a lot more to contribute to rock as she continues her broader search to find a bridge between holistic thinking and subversive reasoning."

The legend was back . . . and she wasn't going anywhere.

8

"DON'T SAY NOTHING"

1997–2000

"Prosperity, progression, persistence" sounds like a mediocre slogan for a high school presidential hopeful. However, these three words can easily describe the status of the United States as well as Patti's career at the dawn of 1997. In January 1997, President Bill Clinton was inaugurated for his second term, becoming the first Democratic incumbent since Lyndon Johnson to be reelected. That same month, Madeleine Albright became the first female secretary of state, showing a slow but positive step toward women receiving higher-ranking positions in government.

In a way, *Gone Again* had been Patti's musical "election" back into the ranks of the record-buying public. After her "inauguration," Smith spent most of early 1997 on the road, with dates in Japan, Australia, and Canada, slowly rebuilding her international status. To further shroud the air of loss that *Gone Again* so expertly conveyed, Smith had to deal with yet another loss during her newly found renaissance. On April 5, 1997, Allen Ginsberg passed away at the age of seventy from a heart attack stemming from complications from liver cancer. Smith was a mainstay at Ginsberg's side during this time, as were many of his friends and closest confidantes. A few days after his passing, Smith performed at his memorial service, held on April 12, 1997, at St. Mark's Church in New York City. Smith joined composer and friend Philip Glass on a reading of the Ginsberg poem "On Cremation of Chogyam Trungpa."

Taking the stage to much applause, Smith breaks the dour mood with a perfectly executed joke. There, before a congregation mourning the loss of a titan of poetic genius, Smith states, "Thank you all for sacrificing the last episode of *Seinfeld* to be here tonight."

After the reading, Smith pointedly tells the audience what Allen had told her when she had experienced the loss of a loved one: "Let go of your loved one and continue your life celebration." Smith suggested to the audience that it let go of Allen, insisting that by fighting the opposing forces of life and continuing to speak freely, it would also be holding onto him.

This theme of "life goes on" is easily depicted on the cover of *Peace and Noise*, the follow-up to *Gone Again*. The cover depicts Smith on a white bed, writing in her notebook. Gone is the sullen widow who resurfaced after all those years on the *Gone Again* cover. Here we see a version of Patti who is back on the scene after suffering more than her fair share of setbacks. The inclusion of Smith writing in her notebook denotes her intentions to get back to work and continue her path. Furthermore, by depicting Smith working on her neatly made bed, the cover connotes the notion that she has musically awoken and is ready to step back up to the plate.

For the first time in their career, Patti and the band decided to produce *Peace and Noise* themselves with the aid of engineer Ray Cicala. The resulting tracks offer a historical overview of politically charged themes and experiences, including the hardships of Dust Bowl refugees, the AIDS epidemic, the Vietnam War, and the Heaven's Gate tragedy. *Peace and Noise* begins with "Waiting Underground," a straight-ahead rock song about the afterlife, the theme of which plays more like a tag to *Gone Again* than the opening track off a new record. From the onset of "Waiting Underground," what is most striking about this song is Smith's authoritative and confident tone, which until that point has not been heard on record since *Easter*. Absent are the varied emotional takes and the heartbroken widow wails heard on *Gone Again*. Instead, we hear Patti with her head held high and ready to command.

The Smith heard on "Waiting Underground" is observing her losses, not through sadness, but through anger. Smith is commenting about the death of her contemporaries, whether they are her late husband, lovers, or friends, and she is through being sad about it. Smith exclaims that there will be a gathering where they will "hammer the earth" with the "beat of their feet," calling on an uprising where the message and manifesto of humanity will be delivered in synchronicity, one step at a time. The drums pull this feeling through the song by firmly delivering an aggressive pulse while the piano trades off from accenting every quarter note to simple melodic flourishes, representing the firm and steady pulse of the human spirit.

The subsequent track, "Whirl Away," is a shining example of bassist Tony Shanahan's work on the record, with his active bass line turning a harmonically static song into an alt-reggae standout. While the harmony remains stationary and utilizes a reggae beat, Shanahan freely moves throughout the song, which Smith picks up on by remaining rhythmically in sync with Shanahan. This calls into the idea of Smith using her voice not as simply a melodic device but as a rhythmic device. She is not concerned about whether you hear a nice melody beneath the music but, rather, the weight of the message behind the words as it plays in concert with her group.

The message that Smith is trying to convey with "Whirl Away" is the senseless nature in which people bastardize life and do away with how precious life is, over the smallest of matters—how people just "whirl away." Smith describes how life can be taken over by the pettiest of circumstances or, in Smith's words, "the color of their skin or the name of their shoes." In a time in her life when she has had to say good-bye to so many, Smith's decree of "why" when it comes to the sanctity of life is both warranted and timely. Smith walks the fine line between concerned citizen and preacher with her lyrics but ultimately ends the song on a positive note by stating "Hello friend" as a way of placing grace on the many "whys" that the world throws upon us.

The album's sole single was "1959," a scathing sentiment of many who question American consumerism, in full bloom at the end of the century. Smith's use of the year 1959 to speak about such issues bear importance, as 1959 was a landmark year for the arts, politics, and the world at large. William Burroughs had published his seminal novel *Naked Lunch*. Allen Ginsberg published his poem "Kaddish," and Miles Davis redefined the jazz ensemble with his album *Kind of Blue*. Politically, John F. Kennedy was informally campaigning for the presidency, and Dr. Martin Luther King visited India to discuss the philosophy of nonviolence with followers of Mahatma Gandhi. In short, the world was changing at a rapid pace on all frontiers.

The sentiment of the song plays into a common viewpoint: as horrific occurrences were happening in the rest of the world, Americans were content to play with their toys. Smith introduces this concept by singing, "Listen to my story, got two tales to tell," mirroring the idea that perspective is an important aspect of the human condition. However well it may be going for one, it may be going equally as bad for the other. Specifically, Smith speaks about the Tibetan Uprising of 1959, where the capital city of Lhasa began to revolt under the dictatorship of China. As a result, mass slaughter, the imprisonment of religious peoples, and other atrocities were carried out. Smith speaks about how little the American people cared about this and were interested only in their late-1950s existence. Smith voices this by singing, "Wisdom and compassion crushed in the land of Shangri-la but in the land of the Impala honey, well we were looking fine," painting a picture that while Tibet was being destroyed by the Chinese, the Americans were sitting pretty in their Chevrolet Impalas.

Perhaps as a means of aligning herself with the Beat poets or in tribute to Ginsberg, Smith adds music to Ginsberg's "Footnote to Howl," resulting in the track "Spell." "Footnote" is the last section from Ginsberg's seminal masterpiece "Howl," a poem that defined the Beat generation and served to introduce Ginsberg as an original literary icon. Perhaps just as important as the content of the poem, "Howl" was considered at the time to be obscene and without artistic merit—to the extent that obscenity charges were brought on its publisher, Lawrence Ferlinghetti of City Lights Books. Ferlinghetti was ultimately found not guilty, and as a result, "Howl" is seen as a victory for free speech and for any artistic pursuit that aims to challenge the status quo.

It's not surprising then that Smith decided to perform this work of Ginsberg, as she at times adopted the bebop-infused rhythm and cadence that many Beat poets adhered to. The music helps to shape and convey the words by not interfering and by remaining static for the most part. As Smith exclaims "Holy" numerous times to ground the rhythm of the song, the meager instrumentation of acoustic guitar, percussion, bass, and guitar effects builds an ethereal soundscape that Smith effortlessly uses to transition between paying tribute to Ginsberg and making the words her own.

The anger that Smith is willing to employ for *Peace and Noise* reaches its apex with the song "Dead City," an in-your-face indictment on the

1990s generation and its innate and hollow shortcomings. Smith's lyrics reflect how she viewed the youth of this era, who waste their time "buildin' scenes on empty dreams and smokin' them one by one." Smith sees that the generation has grown complacent in its viewpoints and actions, especially compared to Smith's generation of progressive politics and forward-thinking actions. Smith, in a most deserved moment of dishing life lessons, calls on this generation by stating, "Ha! You don't need me?" as if to get right up in its face and say, "You need me now more than ever!"

While such a viewpoint could easily be viewed as negative or suggest the despair of the youth of the 1990s, Smith communicates this sentiment through anger by using drawls and vocal rasps to impart her anger so much so that it sounds as if she is on the brink of hurting or nauseating herself. Smith is calling out the 1990s generation to get up and rise against the false hope of a capitalist society. The band mirrors this passion by adding crescendos on the especially biting lyrics, as in Smith's exclamation "With their broken schemes and their lotteries." The band increases the dynamics to sell Smith's anger and despair for a generation that longs to be free in a parasitic society.

Smith quickly changes aural qualities by going from the aggressive "Dead City" into the sullen, introspective "Blue Poles," named after a famed painting by Jackson Pollock. In it, Smith turns our attention to the plight of those who were a part of the Dust Bowl, a period in the 1930s where severe dust storms brought drought to many areas of the United States. As a result, many Americans were forced to leave their homes and migrate west to find work. Smith sings about the circumstances of the Dust Bowl and the heartache of those who left their homes in the Midwest to find a new life out west. Smith abandons metaphor—save for one exception—and other compositional devices to directly tell the story of their hardships and heartache.

Smith tells the story by framing the lyrics as a letter to her mother. Smith paints a picture of the dust-ridden terrain by comparing the dust to "a plague," that "it covered everything" and eventually took the life of Hal, who we can assume is her brother or significant other within her lyrical framework. Smith writes to her mother that "Hal died in my arms," and she writes that blue poles are "infinitely winding." Smith's naming the song after Pollock's painting warrants a comparison. Pollock was a practitioner of "abstract expressionism," a school of thought where the end product is a result of spontaneous creation. One of Pollock's most famous techniques was the swirl of dripping colors, resulting in a rich plethora of color that one can get lost in. Smith's stating that blue poles are "infinitely winding" suggests that her character in the song is lost among a maze of colors or an abstract myriad of life.

An article for *Billboard Magazine* mentions that the song "Death Singing" is about the AIDS epidemic as told through "the description of a final concert by a musician stricken with the disease." Smith compares the image of the musician to death itself by singing, "Have you seen death singing?" conjuring the image of the musician's body being drained of the life that it once had and its time being limited. Musically, the song reflects this by not having a chorus but merely a verse that goes back and forth between an F major chord and an A minor chord. This sparse harmonic implication results in the image of the musician being void of that spark, void of that anthem that once propelled one's existence.

The strength of the band is best heard on the track "Memento Mori," a ten-minute track that was completely improvised in the studio. The song is a musical diatribe about the Vietnam War, with Smith reciting a poem about the fictional "Johnny" on top of the music. What makes the track so compelling is how the band creates a fully realized aural experience, with certain instruments mirroring parts of the story. Daugherty's snare drum rolls represent the sound of a helicopter, which is accented when needed, for example, when Smith recites the line "The copter went up in flames." The guitar represents the fire as a result of the helicopter crash by use of a guitar pedal that creates swooshing sounds. Smith throughout the song sounds more and more angry, perhaps as a way of portraying the voices of those who had become jaded with the state of the war. Smith and the band build the song by slowly increasing the dynamics throughout it, getting louder and louder and mirroring the escalating violence of the Vietnam War until reaching its climax, where we are left with guitar feedback, representing the haze and mess in which the war left the country.

Smith caps the album with the song "Last Call," a song that turns the mass suicide held by the Heaven's Gate cult into a modern fairy tale. Smith takes the event of its mass suicide that occurred on March 26, 1997, as the impetus of the song. Using a third-person narrative of the "young man," Smith tells the story of how he died by singing the real-world implications of the suicide. When she sings, "His face covered over in a mansion high," Smith alludes to how the cult members induced asphyxiation by putting plastic bags over their heads. The song is framed as a cautionary tale, which Smith denotes by stating that everyone, including Christ, wants to be a part of something, but one should not worship false idols and we should "acknowledge all man as fellow creation." The album concludes on a haunting note, with Michael Stipe singing, "Don't be led away" as the band fades to the song's ultimate conclusion.

Critics were vocal about the album's persistence to rise above Smith's recent loss. Greg Kot of the *Chicago Tribune* stated, "On *Peace and Noise*, the quick follow-up, she rocks harder and pushes beyond her personal grief. She surveys a world without compassion, and responds with pleas for kindness that sound a touch too simplistic for a poet of her magnitude." David Fricke of *Rolling Stone* echoes this thought in his review by stating, "Compared with the fragile intimacy of *Gone Again*, *Peace and Noise* is stern in mood, often gruff in tone."

Robert Christgau of the *Village Voice* gives the album an honorable mention in his "Consumer Guide" but calls out the overtly serious tone of the album by stating, "Good thing she's still a little nuts, because funny's beyond or beneath her." *Billboard Magazine* reflected this by stating, "With mainstream rock as hermetic as it is, Smith is unlikely to find acceptance for this highly deserving album outside her loyal college and triple-A core."

Peace and Noise would ultimately reach number 152 on *Billboard Magazine*'s Top 200. In a beautiful reflection of Smith's influence, the album's single "1959" was nominated for a Grammy Award in 1998 in the category of "Best Female Rock Vocal Performance." In the same category was Fiona Apple's "Criminal," Meredith Brook's "Bitch," Ani DiFranco's "Shy," and Abra Moore's "Four Leaf Clover," showing the contemporary music scene that among the new guard of female rock music, Patti Smith was still valid, was still here, and still had more to say.

The remainder of 1997 saw Patti performing regionally, as she was committed to raising Jackson and Jesse without the pressure of constant touring. The fall of 1997 showed Patti using her music to support causes close to her heart. Around the same time that *Peace and Noise* was released, Smith contributed her rendition of the Christmas traditional

"We Three Kings" as a part of the compilation album *A Very Special Christmas 3*, with the sales of the album benefiting the Special Olympics.

In November 1997, Capitol Records released the *Tibetan Freedom Concert*, a series of concerts recorded live in June 1997 on Randall's Island, New York, in an effort to raise awareness of the plight of the Tibetan people. Of the set that Patti performed at the concert, "About a Boy" was included on the album, as well as songs by Radiohead, Beck, and the Beastie Boys. The summer of 1998 proved to be Patti's most active touring cycle of the past few years. Beginning with four concerts at New York's Bowery Ballroom, Patti and the band jet-set across the world with stops in Austria, Hungary, Belgium, Australia, and New Zealand, ultimately ending the year with return to the Bowery Ballroom.

For the group's next album, Patti enlisted the help of producer Gil Norton. The British-born producer had made a name for himself in the alternative scene by producing albums for the Pixies, Pere Ubu, and Foo Fighters. For the cover to *Gung Ho*, Smith decided not to have her image front and center but rather an image of her father as a young serviceman during World War II. Smith stumbled across the photo while looking through his possessions. Smith showed the photo to her mother, who responded by saying, "Look at your father, he was so gung ho." Liking how that sounded, Smith immediately knew that it would be the title of her new record. Additionally, Smith stated that the album's titular song is about Ho Chi Minh, the prime minister of Vietnam, and his bravery in trying to build a free Vietnam. Smith equated him to Gunga Din, which, when their names are juxtaposed, plays off the phrase "gung ho."

Gung Ho carries the idea of progressive thinking and social progression with an alarming sense of enthusiasm and eagerness. Much in the way that her generation had to deal with the Vietnam War and the stench of the Watergate Scandal, the America of the late 1990s was knee-deep in the controversy of President Bill Clinton's impeachment. In a November 1998 article from *Rolling Stone* titled "The Clinton Conversation," Patti voiced that Clinton's impeachment and the subsequent controversy proved to be "more depressing than Watergate," adding that it revealed the growing dissolution of privacy. Smith adds, "We have forced President Clinton to publicly and privately strip himself totally naked before his wife, his child and their whole world, made him go into himself as a human being, examine his heart, examine his behavior and examine his whole self. We asked him to do that—without asking anything of ourselves."

Smith begins the album with a rebel yell of sorts with the song "One Voice," written in memory of Mother Teresa. In it, Smith calls for positive social combat by stating that deep inside all of us is a kernel of kindness that is waiting to blossom. By exclaiming, "In fertile mind there lies the dormant seed," Smith addresses how no matter what state of mind you are in, the conception of compassion is just waiting to be unearthed. Smith further describes this "seed" as being noteworthy to one's sense of humanity, by describing its growth resulting in "charity."

The call-to-arms spirit of "One Voice" was needed during this time in American politics and policy. "One Voice" foreshadowed the 2000 U.S. presidential elections where Vice President Al Gore won the popular vote but Texas governor George W. Bush won the electoral vote and ultimately the presidency. The aftermath stained the American political process and proved ammunition for conspiracy theories, party hatred, and bureaucratic criticisms. However, Smith's lyrics foreshadowed how we may all have one single voice, but together we can make "one voice" and cut through the clutter and noise. The band reflects this in its own way during the verses, with Kaye performing a riff that cuts perfectly through the mix so that his voice can be heard. The blend of Patti's voice with the mix of her band perfectly aims to imply the idea of equality among people.

"Lo and Beholden" showcases a more playful depiction of religious imagery than what Patti normally displays by casting herself as the biblical figure Salome, from a story in the New Testament. In it, Salome's stepfather, Herod Antipas, asks her to dance for him at a banquet and promises her anything that she asks for in return. Prompted by her mother, Herodias, who had been angered that St. John the Baptist had criticized her marriage, Salome asks for the baptist's head. Smith employs a seductive drawl as a means of channeling Salome and welcomes the listener into her state of mind by singing, "I was alone and content in my world." Smith lyrically follows the story before resolving the task of beheading John the Baptist by singing, "The royal word has passed the prophet's head is all I ask." Although the lyrics paint the obvious picture of Salome, the alternative take is the allegory of what

Smith is truly lo and beholden to—art itself—that what might ultimately cost her her "head" is her dedication to the very art form that she has already given so much for.

The band plays off of Smith's seductive take on Salome by trying to be musically alluring, with a guitar providing heavy accents on the off-beats, a sitar-like guitar solo in the middle of the track, and the use of harp throughout the song. Smith's sultry background vocals ultimately give the song its heavenly feel, as if the whole point of the song is to tempt or entice the listener with her magnetism.

Religious icon as metaphor continues with "Boy Cried Wolf," a sharp-tongued criticism of people's need to build saviors and subsequently destroy them. Smith points out that this is not an old story by any means by singing, "Oh the story's told, been told, retold from the sacred scriptures to the tabloids." The lyrics call out the martyr St. Sebastian, who was killed during the Roman emperor Diocletian's persecution of Christians. According to legend, he was rescued and healed by Irene of Rome after being tied to a tree and shot with numerous arrows. Smith calls on this story to indicate our culture's obsession with celebrity, which leads us to immediately turn our attention from our idols to want to feast on "the blood the blood the sacramental blood." Smith contextualizes that any such obsession is an element of the human condition and is one of the many ebbs and flows through the "human tide."

The remnants of Fred's compositional output are heard on the song "Persuasion," which lists Fred as the coauthor. The song has the feeling of being an outtake from *Dream of Life*, with its reverb-drenched riff that plays throughout. Thematically, Smith frames the idea of love being something that one cannot plan but something that just happens through an arbitrary fashion, or as Smith states, love "recruits hearts with its timeless rhythm."

As a love song, "Persuasion" lacks the normal conventions that one associates with love. The song eschews the normal caveats of love by removing the popular puppy-dog concept and instead relying on its real-world implications. Smith discusses the age-old idea of the validity of life without love by positing, "What is the body that has nobody?" warranting the thought of what is the point of life without love? However, Smith is eager to point out that while this may be the case that there is no structure to how true love occurs, "what is the system that's no system at all?" The song benefits greatly from Smith's vocal delivery, which at times is tonally Dylan-esque and at other times is purposefully milquetoast to mirror the arbitrary nature of true love.

The upbeat, noirish "Gone Pie" balances the themes of light and dark by representing the light with an upbeat chorus and the dark via a guitar riff in the verse that sounds like it was on the soundtrack to a campy noir film. In the beginning of the song, Smith breaks the musical fourth wall by directly addressing the listeners with a sultry "hey there," inviting them into her world. During the verse, Smith speaks of taking a walk "until the dawn is gone," painting a picture of a nighttime stroll with her new companion, the listener. The music supports this feeling of darkness with the guitar riff and with the keyboard producing a Theremin-like sound resulting in an eerie mood.

Upon reaching the chorus, the song completely changes feeling upon Smith singing, "Strolling, ain't it wonderful into a light that lingers." The lingering light in question represents the idea of a spiritual light or even the light that one might encounter on one's way to the afterlife. But Smith does not linger on this notion for too long, as she ends the song on a life-affirming note by repeating the phrase "May you live a long life" three times, resulting in a positive conclusion.

Gung Ho returns to the notion of love and loss with "China Bird," a delicate, midtempo ballad that is delicate in its execution and appealing in its simplicity. Vocally, the song can be seen as the kissing cousin to "My Madrigal" from *Gone Again*. Both are vocally demanding, closely treading the line between heartfelt emotion and melodramatic candor. Musically, both take a chordal instrument and use it as the foundation of the song with the rest of the ensemble joining in at a later date. With "My Madrigal," the piano is the foundation, and with "China Bird" the guitar is the foundation, both resulting in different timbral qualities but with similar emotional responses. This creates a musical swelling, which aids to increase the overall emotional tone of the song by slowly adding layers for the listeners to digest, as opposed to throwing everything at them at once.

Smith uses the phrase "China bird" as a metaphor for the form one takes when the heavens are opening their doors to the dearly departed. Smith sings, "You China bird the open skies are yearning for you," invoking the idea that heaven is opening its arms to welcome the recently deceased. Smith conceives that if the heavens themselves reject the departed, her love will help you ascend to them. By singing, "If they say it's not your way, hold your view with my love fly above," Smith invokes this idea.

Smith calls out corporate consumerism and commercialism with the track "Glitter in Their Eyes," a frenetic rocker that is the cornerstone of the album. Smith bitterly calls out the glorified materialism of Generation Y and how twentysomethings have become the ultimate commodity to the corporate culture they celebrate. Smith harshly expresses her angst by stating, "They'll trade you up trade you down, your body's a commodity," using the idea of one's body and temple as a marketing tool by corporate America. Smith easily lets her disdain for such commercialism shine through her vocal delivery, at times flippant although forceful. The production of the song echoes the idea of "glitter" during the chorus, with the ethereal, reverb-drenched delivery of the line "Oh can't you see the glitter, the glitter in their eyes."

Smith also uses "Glitter in Their Eyes" as a way of taking a trip down memory lane in an uncharacteristic bit of nostalgia about a specific location that she hasn't yet taken on record. Smith gibes that the "Dow is jonesing at the bit, 42nd Disney Street," calling into the Disneyfication of Times Square that occurred during the Rudolph Giuliani's tenure as the mayor of New York City. Smith calls this out by letting the listeners know that among the "glitter" that twinkles "is not all that glitters" and that they should look inward to find their true "glitter."

Patti's axe to grind ventures into racial inequality and lineage with "Strange Messengers," an angst-ridden message about slavery that ventures dangerously toward rhetoric. Smith takes the form of a specter, peering over a landscape as she sings, "Looking down at their naked feet bound in chains," describing the atrocity of human enslavement. What's kept unclear is whether Smith has cast herself as the specter of a slave or a casual observer, as the lyric blurs the line between the two opposing forces: "We knew it was wrong but we looked away and paraded them down the colonial streets." By blurring the lines between slave and bystander, Smith is representing a historical sampling of the populous, which runs the fine line between property and punishment. What is clear is that Smith starts to paint a picture of complacency and atrocity as being a long-standing scab on the human condition.

Toward the latter half of the song, Smith's admonition toward contemporary African American men is borderline insulting, as she shouts,

"Smoking crack, crack! That's how you pay your ancestors? All those dreams go up in your pipe, up in smoke?" In his review of *Gung Ho* for *Slant Magazine*, Sal Cinquemani points out Smith's outcry only scratches the surface of the underlying problem: "Her lyrics imply that poverty-stricken black people are selfish and ungrateful of their ancestry rather than the product of a racist, dysfunctional society." Smith's finger-pointing eventually undercuts an epidemic that she has shown to be both historical and contemporary. While Cinquemani's take on "Strange Messengers" is warranted, Smith's mere inclusion of this on the record shows that a major artist is not going to stand by and let a minority continue to suffer in historical contexts and contemporary mores.

Through the political haze that Smith has woven at this point in *Gung Ho*, she takes a step back to take stock of life with the song "Grateful." The song was written soon after the sessions for *Gone Again* were completed, and it was inspired in part by the late Grateful Dead singer/guitarist Jerry Garcia. After a particularly melancholy afternoon, Smith closed her eyes and pictured Garcia standing before her winking at her while pulling one of his gray hairs.

The major theme that Smith tries to convey with "Grateful" is the concept of death being not only an inevitable occurrence but an event that is just one of many that people experience. Smith opens the song by stating, "Ours is just another skin that simply slips away," conjuring the idea that life will end, not through great pain, but with relative ease. Smith shows her survivalist mentality by assuring the listener, "It all will come out fine, I've learned it line by line," warranting the idea she has learned quite a bit about death and that it will ultimately be okay.

Smith's continued call for reaction and response from a divided populous is heard loud and clear on "Upright Come." Smith employs a Morrison-esque tone while trying to sing the passion of life into an apathetic society, with such commands as "Awake people, arise!" Smith employs nouns that one might associate with the laidback lifestyle of the 1960s and 1970s by starting several phrases with "hail brother" and "hail sister." However, any comparisons to the free-love movement end here, as she calls out her own generation by scowling, "Wasted icons, wasted lives like war obsolete." The "wasted lives" in question could mean any set of lives, but given the time frame of the album and the reference to the "war" (the Vietnam War), the wasted lives could very well indicate

Hendrix and Morrison or any of her fellow comrades of her generation that have passed on.

Smith sustains the soapbox pleasantries with the funk-fueled manifesto "New Party." With a beginning guitar riff that sounds lifted from the Red Hot Chili Peppers, Smith shows a musically looser side that she doesn't normally reveal. This looseness bleeds into the lyrical arc of the song, with Smith playing with the rhythm of the words in the Ginsbergian sense by employing growls, pauses, and other vocal techniques.

The overly political agenda of the song collapses the lyrical capacity of the song with Smith relying more on slogan than substance. Assertions such as "I think we're gonna need a new party" and "We got to get off our ass or get burned" feel too simple and lacking the bite that has come to define Smith's lyrical output. However, Smith's comparison of politicians' words with fertilizer ("Why don't you fertilize my lawn with what's running from your mouth?") offers a much-needed joke in an otherwise serious album.

Smith pays tribute to Elizabeth Bacon Custer, General George Custer's wife, with the song "Libbie's Song." During the Civil War, General Custer was seen in a negative light after the Battle of the Little Bighorn took his life and the lives of more than 250. Elizabeth spent the remainder of her life dedicated to clearing her husband's name and vindicating his life and career. Smith casts herself in the role of Elizabeth and portrays the love that she feels for her husband, especially during the Battle of the Little Bighorn. Smith sings, "You marched proudly for the horn, I prayed for your swift return," conveying the idea that Elizabeth above all was proud and supportive of her husband. The bluegrass-infused textures of acoustic guitar, violin, and mandolin give the instrumentation a deeply personal ambiance, aided by the vulnerability that Smith expresses with her voice.

Gung Ho ends with the album's title track, a reflection on perhaps the biggest scar that affected people of Patti's generation: the Vietnam War. The song begins with the guitar lingering on an E chord, which remains constant throughout the song, ultimately acting as the song's pulse. The sparse drum pattern, echo-infused rhythm guitar, and Smith's reverb-touched voice adds on overall hazy feeling, as it we were on the front lines of the war. The introduction also feels like a more coherent introduction to the Doors's "The End," with Smith adding her own Morrison-esque vocal articulations to the song.

The importance of the Vietnam War to Smith's generation cannot be undervalued, as it was a constant source of cultural and political upheaval for those coming of age on the mid-1960s to the mid-1970s. This idea of a constant takes the form of the guitar playing the E chord and the soft-spoken chants of "Gung Ho" in the background, as if the war was constantly breathing down your neck, constantly on your mind. In addition to the static E chord played throughout the song, background helicopter noises are heard, filling in the percussive gap of the drums and adding a sense of anxiety to the song, ultimately ending *Gung Ho* on a musical cliffhanger as if to say "Where do we go from here?"

The title track is also rumination on Ho Chi Minh, the revolutionary and former president of North Vietnam. The idea for the song came while Smith watched a documentary on Ho Chi Minh during a tour in Australia. Not knowing much about him, Smith was taken by the fact that Ho Chi Minh knew more about American history than she did, having used the U.S. Declaration of Independence as his model for Vietnam. Inspired by this, Smith began to study Ho Chi Minh extensively, as well as American history. Her study and the song helped her acknowledge the effects of the Vietnam War and the lives it took.

Reviews for *Gung Ho* were fairly positive but ranged from glowing to tepid to flat-out acid tongued. David Browne from *Entertainment Weekly* gave the album an A and stated, "As for that voice—a fierce if unvarnished instrument—Smith has never sounded better. She sings with both a new vigor (a burnished snarl has crept into her voice) and a new tenderness." Keith Phipps from the *AV Club* contextualizes that of the three albums released during this time, *Gung Ho* is Smith's "most direct and, not coincidentally, hardest-rocking album since 1978's *Easter.*" Michael Sandlin at *Pitchfork Media* was less than enthusiastic about the album and was quick to point out that a lot of her music at this time was influenced by the tragedy in her life. Sandlin states, "True, she's endured some personal tragedies along the way—namely, the untimely death of both her husband and brother. But the real tragedy, I'd say, is her growing inability to write a decent song." Sandlin spreads the wealth of dismay by stating, "And as Patti's ideas dwindle, her faithful band follows suit with typically bland, unchallenging classic rock gestures. Sure, Lenny Kaye is still capable of penning a clever riff here and there, but mostly, he just follows the notes and pockets his paycheck."

Scathing reviews aside, the album reached number 178 on *Billboard Magazine*'s Top 200 and warranted her second Grammy Award nomination for "Best Female Rock Vocal Performance," for "Glitter in Her Eyes." Perhaps the biggest result for *Gung Ho* was the use of "New Party" as the campaign song for Green Party candidate Ralph Nader's 2000 presidential bid. In conversation with Greg King for *The Sun*, Smith stated, "I consider Ralph Nader the greatest of patriots, because he lives by our organic law and has spent his life serving the people. I would hope I share some of his kind of patriotism."

Nader proved his popularity among the younger generation by doing what few politicians have ever done or will ever do . . . sell out Madison Square Garden. On October 13, 2000, Patti participated in "Ralph Rocks the Garden," a show at the famed New York City venue that benefited Nader's campaign. Alongside musicians Ani DiFranco, Eddie Vedder, and Ben Harper, as well as actors Susan Sarandon, Bill Murray, and Tim Robbins, the evening showcased people who were ready for a change, ready to take action. The evening ended with all the acts coming together to sing "People Have the Power," capping off with a sense of hope that was longed for. Smith later stated, "It's not all over, they didn't do it all in the '60s, it's not nostalgia. We can reclaim the ability and the right to use our collective voice."

After five years, three albums, two Grammy nominations, and countless touring, Smith proved that in the mid- to late 1990s, much in the way that she spoke of the collective voice of the 1960s, she did not do it all. The subsequent years would arguably be Smith's most high-profile time in her career.

9

"NEW PARTY"

2001–2009

With the dawn of the new millennium, America and the world at large were fluttering with all things new. The American people were given a clean slate, the chance to shake off the Y2K dust, to eschew the impeachment of Bill Clinton, and to move forward as a nation. While the promise of a fresh start kept the American people frothing with anticipation, the first blow in the renewal of American optimism was the debacle over the 2000 presidential election between Al Gore and George W. Bush. The second and generation-defining blow occurred on the morning of September 11, 2001.

On that morning, nineteen terrorists hijacked four commercial airliners, with two crashing into the north and south towers of the World Trade Center, one crashing into the Pentagon, and the fourth crashing into a field in Shanksville, Pennsylvania, en route to the White House. The event shook the very foundation of America's core, increasing the anxieties of the American people. In response, Smith participated in the public discourse about the events, not through expressions of hate or anger, but through her art. Not a month after September 11, Smith performed at the Poetry Project's event titled "New Poems to End Greed, Imperialism, Opportunism and Terrorism: Poets Respond to the September 11th Attacks and Ensuing Events."

Smith delved within herself and responded with the journal entry/ poem titled "Twin Death," where she compared the heap of rubble

where the Twin Towers once stood to the skeleton remains of humanity. Smith contextualizes, "I see their skeletal remains, resembling
Brueghel's portrait of Babel. Atop them, two twisted fingers reach hea-
venward in the perfect shape of a V. The simple sign for Peace." Smith
affectively takes the result of a hateful act by simultaneously mourning
its loss and championing the aftermath as a sign of love and reconcilia-
tion.

While the nation was clamoring to rebuild itself in its time of need,
Smith continued to move ahead with several new projects. On March
19, 2002, Arista Records released *Land (1975–2002)*, a two-disc compilation album that acts as part greatest hits, part b-sides, and part live
album. While the first disc contains classic songs from her catalog, the
second contains materials picked by her fans. Smith noted in the press
release for *Land*, "I have always cherished the energy and input of
audiences during our live performances, and I thought it would be
more interesting if this CD were to reflect the actual ideas of the people
who listen to our music. So I invited their input, by asking people to
send a list of their own favorite songs to me." In his review for *Rolling
Stone*, David Fricke mentions how *Land* showcased her commitment to
art and to its long-lasting effects: "This two-record set distills Patti
Smith's rock & roll life into seventeen classic tracks, fourteen studio and
live rarities and two basic truths: There is no revolution without toil, and
no euphoria without communion." It would also be Smith's last release
on Arista Records.

After twenty-five years with Arista Records, Smith found herself at a
crossroads. Patti likened herself to baseball Hall of Famer Al Kaline,
who spent the entirety of his career with the Detroit Tigers. Smith
commented, "I get on one team, and that's the team I like to have." On
October 20, 2002, on what would have been Arthur Rimbaud's 148th
birthday, Smith signed to Columbia Records, home to everyone from
Bob Dylan and Bruce Springsteen to Miles Davis. Not long after, Smith
and the band began developing material for their next album, entitled
Trampin'.

One may argue that *Trampin'* is Smith at her most outspoken. With
songs about spirituality, motherhood, and the American spirit, Smith's
voice has never had so many topics that it was looking to address and
with such authority and vigor. With *Trampin'* Smith aimed to capture

the post–September 11 landscape through the lens of artist, mother, and American—three distinct voices housed within one woman.

The album cover for *Trampin'* continues with what the album cover of *Gung Ho* started with: Smith deliberately not putting her face on the cover nor using a different form of iconography to voice the album's themes. For *Trampin'*, the cover photo depicts Smith's foot on the ground with her toes slightly out of focus. The idea of a bare foot on the ground may symbolize an idea of stability with the out-of-focus toes referring to a blurring of one's foundation. Alternatively, the idea of feet may represent mobility, independence, and freedom or one's need to contemplate one's goals.

Trampin' begins with the religiosocial anthem "Jubilee," a tribal-influenced jaunt regarding the titular religious concept. In Judaism and Christianity, a "jubilee" is a year that occurs every fifty years where the enslaved or indentured were set free to return to their land and debts were pardoned. As stated in Leviticus 25:8–13, "Consecrate the fiftieth year and proclaim liberty throughout the land to all its inhabitants. It shall be a jubilee for you; each of you is to return to your family property and to your own clan."

The "liberty" spoken of in Leviticus is everpresent in Smith's performance, as she aims to celebrate by proclaiming, "Come on boy, come on girl be a jubilee," not asking but demanding that the listener celebrate with her. "Jubilee" juggles the idea of duality: good/bad, pessimism/optimism. Within the same song, Smith goes from singing, "Scattering our glad day with debt and despair" to "We are love and the future," resulting in a multilayered outlook on her supposed "jubilation." In Smith's execution in representing this duality, she turns jubilation from a religious concept to a personal construct. Smith first sings, "Scattering our glad day with debt and despair" with the soft-spoken air of a damaged bird, sullen and compromised before suddenly obtaining gravitas and shouting, "Come on people gather round, you know what to do," as if the weakness that she was delivering in the prior line was all a ruse to surprise the listener.

Said ruse is all but a footnote on "Mother Rose," where Smith contemplates her standing in the world as both the daughter of a woman and the mother of two children. Smith sings, "Mother rose every little mornin' to tend to me," which shows Smith ruminating on how her mother cared for her in a selfless fashion, waking with her and tending to her needs. Shortly after, Smith literally "turns the view" of the song by switching her perspective from child to mother by singing to her child, "Now's the time to turn the view now that I have you." Smith, with the perspective of being a mother, sings, "And I'll rise every little mornin' to tend to thee," mirroring the love and affection that she experienced through her own mother and using that same love and affection with her children. Smith later sings about the wealth and importance of a mother's love by singing, "She felt our tears, heard our sighs and turned to gold," as if by caring for the childhood ills of her children, Smith's mother was turned into a beautiful, gleaming person that could be compared only to the wealth that gold inhabits. The band serves to reinforce this idea of light and gold by arpeggiating the chords, resulting in a chimelike effect that adds an ethereal tone to the end of the song.

Smith immediately breaks the ethereal tone that she establishes with "Mother Rose" with the bare-bones rock of "Stride of the Mind." Musically, the opening guitar riff sounds like a slowed-down version of the opening riff to the MC5's "Kick Out the Jams," further succeeding in letting the listener know how pertinent Fred is in Patti's life, even after having been deceased for many years. Smith declares that the mind is an instrument of purpose—and a forward-thinking purpose it should serve. To accomplish this, Smith calls on the story of Simeon Stylites, a Christian saint who famously stood atop a pillar for more than thirty-seven years to be as close as he could to God and to lift himself above the concerns of Earth, overpowering the downward tendency of human nature.

Smith speaks of Simeon's pillar by singing, "It's a vertical climb, the climb the climb," invoking the image of Simeon climbing to the top of his pillar to reach the heavens as best he could. One can make the claim that Smith is comparing herself to Simeon, as the pillar could be compared to a concert stage. Such a similarity can be seen in artist Luis Bunuel's take on the story of Simeon with his short film *Simon of the Desert*, which concludes with the devil taking Simon to a rock club where young people are performing a dance called the "radioactive flesh."

The gentle lullaby "Cartwheels" begins with a guitar strumming a chord with a chimelike effect while the bass plays low, with notes creating a vast world that can be perceived as either ethereal or sinister. The lyrics were written for Smith's daughter Jesse and can be interpreted as a mother's sight of her daughter growing up from a small child and into an adult, trying to survey the chaos and insanity of the modern world.

Smith characterizes her daughter's exit as a child and entrance into adulthood by singing, "Spring is departing," comparing the transition between childhood and adulthood to a seasonal change. Furthermore, Smith supports this by stating, "Her thoughts are darting like a rabbit, like a rabbit 'cross the moon,'" characterizing her daughter's thoughts as being of a teenager who changes just as rapidly as a rabbit darting. Smith ultimately lets her daughter know that whatever happens in this world, "Don't let it bring you down," and as the wheels of life continue to turn, she will see her daughter doing "cartwheels."

Smith returns to the necessity of spiritual and political guidance with "Gandhi." Over the course of the nearly ten-minute song, Smith and the band tell the story of Gandhi while slowly crescendoing to a feverish pace, with Smith declaring "Awake from your slumber." Smith begins the song a capella by singing with a strained drawl, "I had a dream Mr. King, if you'll beg my pardon," challenging the memory of Dr. Martin Luther King Jr. by saying that he wasn't the only one that had a dream. It's an audacious beginning but an important one, as it places the memory of both Dr. Martin Luther King Jr. and Gandhi in humanistic terms, making their efforts all the more important as they were manmade. Smith calls on Gandhi to "awake from your slumber and get 'em with the numbers," calling on his memory to help her rally support, perhaps surrendering to the idea that her one voice cannot possibly carry out her mission but that the collective voice has more weight behind it.

The repetitive yet strong performance of the band during "Gandhi" creates this dreamlike, delirious environment. In his review in *PopMatters*, Rob Horning echoes this thought by stating, "The music, with its long, repetitious crescendo is so hypnotizing, it makes it seem as though Smith is suggesting that revolutionary fervor is understood best as a trance state. This makes her stance seem a bit ambiguous, making us wonder if she means to advocate revolution to the point of being committed past the necessity of thought, or reveal revolutionaries as a bit brainwashed, no longer consciously committed to a cause but centripetally sucked into it by an irresistible rhythm, an aural analogue for mob frenzy."

In an album that calls on the memory of spiritual and political leaders of yesterday, the deeply introspective "Trespasses" serves as a palette cleanser from the album's core themes as well as a reminder of the
fragility of life. With the sparse instrumentation of voice, guitar, organ,
and bass, Smith gently begins the song by speaking about how our lives
are controlled by an outside force ("Life is designed with unfinished
lines that another sings"). By comparing life to music, Smith characterizes life as a positive force, something both simple and complex that
follows a narrative arc.

Smith sings, "Each story unfolds like it was gold," generating the
thought that every life is important and worth something. Smith is eager
to voice the sadness and happiness that life can bring. In a dour turn,
Smith sings, "All of my debts left with regrets, I'm sorry for everything,"
revealing that her life has warranted her fair share of anguish. However,
it's through being a mother that Smith has found her happiness. Smith
compares the regrets of one's lifetime to that of a coat, which her son
takes at the end of the song while "joyfully whistling," as if said regret
did not affect him.

While *Trampin'* spends a fair amount of time dealing with the political and religious struggles of people, Smith taps into the artistic struggle
of poet and painter William Blake on the song "My Blakean Year." The
influence of Blake on Smith is long-standing, an influence that she
shared with William Burroughs. In a 2000 interview with *Tate Magazine*, Smith stated, "Burroughs was fond of Blake, and it was just so
simple to him. He said Blake just saw what others did not—and it
seemed like a good answer. I mean, Blake was so generous with his
angels that even we can look at them now."

"My Blakean Year" speaks about the pursuit of faith, spiritual confidence, and garnering acceptance. In his time, Blake was not appreciated for his artistic output, dying penniless and without the accolades he
so deserved. Subsequent to his passing, Blake has become the heralded
hero in death that he never got to become in life. This disparity between success and failure is mirrored in the line "Brace yourself for
bitter flack for a life sublime," creating an image that going through the
dredges, the motions of life will ultimately prove a life worth living.

The idea of a "Blakean Year" establishes a set time in which an
individual can combat the fear that is holding one back. In an interview
with David Fricke from *Rolling Stone*, Smith attributed this fear as

being the Bush administration. Specific to her lyric "Throw off your stupid cloak, embrace all that you fear," Smith states, "The worst thing the Bush administration has done is instill huge amounts of fear in our people. That is deplorable. We have to replace that fear with awareness and a determination to make things better." The lyrical wealth of "My Blakean Year" benefits from the overall pulse of the song, which would normally fall to the drums or rhythm guitar. But on "My Blakean Year," it is satisfied by the incorporating of a cello, which follows the chord structure of A minor, C major, and B minor but performs the song entirely in eight notes, resulting in a steady, unobtrusive pace.

In keeping with the album's tone of reflection and looking inward, "Cash" can be viewed as a song that is the result of a woman that has seen the cyclical nature of life. When *Trampin'* was released, the Bush administration was in full swing, and its policies warranted protest and outrage. Smith saw the same thing happen during the Vietnam War, with the difference being that Smith's generation was not afraid to stand up and speak its mind. While protests regarding the Bush administration occurred, Smith may feel that it's time for this generation to stand up—or, in her words, "Stand among the fallen ones, take revenge defeated sons."

"Peaceable Kingdom" plays on the idea of rebuilding a fractured world through the passage of time. Dedicated to Rachel Corrie, the American peace activist killed by a bulldozer during a protest at the Gaza Strip, the title of the song can be traced to the 1826 painting of the same name by artist Edward Hicks. Hicks gave this title to more than a hundred of his paintings, which depicted gentle and fierce animals coexisting peacefully and usually included a scene depicting William Penn signing a peace treaty with the Indians. "Peaceable Kingdom" serves as an allegorical device, representing the ideal of peaceful coexistence of humankind, rather than an actual scene.

Given the time that *Trampin'* was released, the song can easily be viewed as a rumination on September 11, which had occurred a mere two and a half years before the album's release. Rather than provide a cacophony of noise to represent the pain and confusion of the tragic event, Smith and Co. tell Smith's story through gentle articulations and soft tones. The song begins with a soft swell, with keyboards and the drums playing a gentle march on the snare drum, creating an environment of quiet and calm, much like the morning of September 11 itself.

Smith does not harbor anger or fear but rather faith and hope. Smith gently sings, "Maybe one day we'll be strong enough to build it back again, build the peaceable kingdom back again," acknowledging that we must mourn but at the very least look forward to rebuilding what has been figuratively and actually destroyed. This sentiment is echoed at the close of the song, which ends just as it began, with the keyboard fading out to the sounds of children's laughter, warranting a true completion to the "peaceable kingdom."

While "Peaceable Kingdom" uses children's laughter to express a sense of calm and hope, the use of the same children's laughter at the beginning of "Radio Baghdad" gives the feeling of an imminent storm or something about to burst. Speaking to the *New York Times*, Smith stated that "Radio Baghdad" takes the voice of a mother "trying to sing her child to sleep telling her about the history of her country as the Americans are bombing."

The themes of the song speak of Smith's lyrical description about the city of Baghdad and its culture and ruin resulting from American warmongering and cultural absurdism. To Smith's credit, the song could easily be seen as an antiwar song, but she decides early on to eschew this route and instead delineate Baghdad and its place among American politics.

The many ebbs and flows of the song feel as if it is a part of a larger work, and in that respect, "Radio Baghdad" plays like a suite from the larger work of the album. The opening two minutes have Smith, via spoken word, tell of Baghdad's wartime terrain and how the city's science, mathematics, and engineering feats have been leveled by American policy. The band uses sparse drums, ringing guitar notes, and brief clarinet drones to set the stage for the rest of the song, much in the way that a prelude accomplishes in a classical composition.

Immediately after speaking the phrase "abrasive, aloof," the guitar begins to play a distorted riff that brings on the lyrical storm that Smith hinted at in the introduction. Even inside this musical and lyrical fury that is being presented, Smith speaks of a positive note among it. Smith compares Baghdad as the "center of the world" and that "with its great mosques" it will "rise from the ashes like a speckled bird."

To further clarify how the United States violated Baghdad, Smith speaks of the oil beneath Iraqi soil as blood and how, due to U.S. foreign policy, we drill the earth for profit or, as Smith states, "little droplets of oil for bracelets, little jewels." Smith ends the song much as it began, with soft instrumentation and a declaration that you should not suffer but rather "extend your hand" to your neighbor.

Smith concludes the album with the somber and reflective title track. Consisting of only voice and piano, Smith sings with the earnest realism of a traveler, someone who has been on a long and incredible journey. Smith begins the song by singing, "I'm trampin', trampin' try'n-a make heaven my home," conveying a sense that she is on a long journey toward Heaven. "Try'n-a make heaven my home" can be interpreted as a nod to the gospel hymn "Coming for to Carry Me Home," a song that invokes the image of angels carrying one's soul to Heaven. The title track adds extra brevity with the inclusion of Smith's daughter Jesse on piano, adding an intimate feel to an already personal song.

Critics were quick to mention that *Trampin'* showcased a mellower-sounding Smith but still within her tenacious attitude. Tom Lanham from *Paste Magazine* stated, "a wiser, mellower malcontent—as Smith appears on her new *Trampin'*—with roughly the same amount of *Horses* steam, but delicate, gracious new ways of releasing it." This idea of Smith using new ways to pack a punch was reflected in the BBC's review when critic Chris Jones said, "Aesthetically, *Trampin'* is an album that's a million miles away from the barbed wire urgency of *Horses*, yet lyrically and in spirit it's as urgent and insistent as ever."

Not all were excited about *Trampin'*. Zac Pennington in the *Portland Mercury*, while praising the record for its post–September 11 slice of American life, questioned Smith's relevance in contemporary society: "And though Smith's politics are certainly more beautifully articulated than that of nearly any other political reactionary in music today, it's still a little difficult to stomach a fifty-seven-year-old rock star mom harping on (over a largely flaccid classic rock band) about civil liberties, shock and awe, Martin Luther King, Ghandi, and, most offensively, 'us' versus 'them'—regardless of her conviction."

In the summer of 2005, Smith was named the director of London's Meltdown Festival, an annual festival where a musician is asked to program the festival in its entirety with the artists and musicians of their choice. Past artists have included everyone from avant-garde composer Louis Andriessen, singer Morrissey, and free jazz pioneer Ornette Coleman. As part of her duties, Smith programmed a festival that featured her eclectic tastes, including singer-songwriter Billy Bragg, guitarist Fred Frith, harpist Joanna Newsom, and guitarist John Frusciante, to name a few.

For the festival, Smith had to look outside herself and be social in a way that she was not entirely comfortable with. Speaking to *The Guardian*, Smith spoke of the festival as being "the most social experience of my life." In a beautifully humble expression of beauty and grace, Smith stated, "I will now have to totally immerse myself in a way I have never done. I tend to be insular and opinionated. But for this, I want to, and will, work alongside people. I'll perform myself, but if anyone else needs a bit of backing vocal, clarinet or a shirt ironed, I'll be there." What was most important about Smith's duties as a programmer was her inclusion of her own band performing *Horses* in its entirety in commemoration of its thirty-year anniversary.

When scenes and movements become mainstream, it's only fitting that the public lift them up beyond their means to great new heights. Consequently, when the major players of a scene began to fade and break free from this mortal coil, we see the true fabric of the scene. For the scene that began at CBGB, that fabric began to uncoil on April 15, 2001, with the death of Ramones lead singer Joey Ramone. This was only the beginning, as CBGB founder Hilly Kristal succumbed to lung cancer on August 28, 2007. Perhaps one of the most significant blows came on October 15, 2006, when CBGB closed its doors for good.

To commemorate its closing, Smith and the band performed two sets. Beginning at 9:30 pm on October 15, Smith performed her songs as well as songs by other bands made famous by CBGB, including Television's "Marquee Moon" (which featured Lloyd on guitar), Blondie's "The Tide Is High," the Dead Boys' "Sonic Reducer," and a Ramones medley sung by Kaye. During the evening, Smith was quick to point out Kristal's legacy: "This place that Hilly so generously offered to us to create new ideas, to fail, to make mistakes, to reach new heights."

Smith rounded out the set with "Elegie" and read a list of dead punk rock musicians and advocates that had graced the CBGB community. Upon speaking about where the next generation will go to express its music, Smith insisted, "They'll find a place that nobody wants, and you got one guy who believes in you, and you just do your thing. And anybody can do that, anywhere in the world, any time."

Smith's legacy as a rock-and-roll icon was solidified on March 12, 2007, when she was inducted into the Rock and Roll Hall of Fame.

With a class that included hip-hop pioneers Grandmaster Flash and the Furious Five, college rock pioneers REM, pop rockers Van Halen, and girl group the Ronettes, Smith's induction marked a stamp of approval from the industry that she both fought against and was an active member of. Singer Zach de la Rocha of the band Rage against the Machine inducted Smith and delivered a speech not only celebrating her career but also highlighting the importance of her voice: "The opening to 'Gloria' might be one of the greatest moments in American Music. And then you hear that voice, and you think 'Nothing could be this haunting and nothing could be this healing at the same time.'"

Appearing humbled, Smith stood at the podium and thanked those who shepherded her throughout her life, the musicians both past and present who touched her life, the crew who kept her wheels in motion, her children and those in her life she no longer has. Smith ended her speech with an anecdote about Fred and how one evening they were having an argument in their kitchen while Smith was peeling potatoes. Fred stated, "Tricia, one day you're going to get into the Rock and Roll Hall of Fame," to which Patti shooed him away. Fred then said, "Yes you will and you're not going to like it or you might feel rebellious, or you might feel guilty 'cause I'm not in it and I'm clearly the better one."

As is custom with the induction ceremony, the entire class of that year jams on a song, with Smith's "People Have the Power" being the song that everyone played on. Smith was especially moved to perform the song, as it was a way to cap off the night, seeing that her late husband wrote the music, with Smith contributing the lyrics, and it would have been moving for Fred to see everybody sing the song together.

When it came time to record her follow-up to *Trampin'*, Smith decided to record an album of covers. Artists covering other artist's songs are a long-standing tradition in popular music circles. A cover, when done right and in the right hands, transcends the intent of the original and takes on a new life with a new meaning. A proper cover takes the familiarity and routine of an established song and adds a new spin, a new way of experiencing the song that can introduce it to an entirely new generation.

Twelve comes from a long line of covers records. David Bowie's last album as his alter ego Ziggy Stardust was 1973's *Pin Ups*, where he covered popular songs by the Who and the Kinks. John Lennon's last album before going on a family sabbatical was 1975's *Rock 'n' Roll*, where he covered early rock-'n'-roll songs that he cherished as a young man, including "Be-Bop-a-Lula," written by Tex Davis and Gene Vincent, and "Ain't That a Shame," by Fats Domino.

Smith returns to form with *Twelve*, as covers—or her take on what cover songs can achieve—are riddled throughout her career. From *Horses* through *Twelve*, Smith used covers as a way of piercing her influences with her own spin and style. From "Gloria," to "So You Want to Be a Rock 'n' Roll Star" to "Wicked Messenger," Smith has utilized covers as a way of expressing her talents. Regarding *Twelve*, Smith stated, "I want to do justice to the person's song. Often, I'll pick a song that I envy. Or one that moves me so much that I want to try it myself. I also try to add another dimension to each song. Another goal of mine was to present the songs in a certain way that you could really get the lyrics. So, a lot of my attention for this record was focused on the inner narrative. It was to present these songs lyrically."

The liner notes of *Twelve* speak of an album of cover songs being in the works as far back as 1978, but Smith felt that she still had more to learn about singing and lacked the experience necessary to do such an undertaking. Additionally, the album itself has a more practical purpose, more of a series of etudes to challenge her voice, as opposed to a curation of a series of songs for the sake of doing so. Speaking to Len Rigi of Popmatters.com, Smith stated, "I really did this record as an exercise in singing, and singing well." Furthermore, Smith told Rigi that she doesn't consider herself a talented singer and, when asked why, stated, "I know the difference between a natural singer and what I can do. Joan Osborne, Joan Baez, Emmylou Harris—they trill like birds."

When it came time to select the playlist, Smith found it difficult to choose which songs she wanted to cover, seeing as her tastes and imagination were constantly changing. Smith ended up recording six from an initial list and an additional six that found their way onto the list during the recording process. Smith ended up recording the songs lyrically untouched. She made the conscious decision not to alter any of the lyrics or add to the lyrics, as she did earlier in her career with "Gloria" and "Land of a Thousand Dances." Smith stated that the legal headache that came with such an idea was too much: "A lot of artists don't want their music expanded, and so if you do it, they can stop your record. I decided I didn't want to get involved in a lot of heartbreaking legal entanglements."

Smith begins *Twelve* with her take on the classic psychedelic rock anthem "Are You Experienced?" written by Jimi Hendrix. From the onset of the record, Smith knew that Hendrix would be included on it. Speaking to *MSN Music*, Smith stated, "He was a great performer, beautiful, intense, a great lyricist, even a great dresser. So I chose the song I felt in the past I was not qualified to do—when I would ask myself, 'Are you experienced?' the answer was always, 'No, I'm not.' And at this time in my life, I felt like I knew enough and had been through enough to tackle the song."

The song's central theme of internal peace and being open to experience rings true in Smith's life. Smith, in contrast, strips the song down to a sexual provocation, frank and direct—powerful stuff coming from a woman who at this time was well into her sixties, who has survived many summers of love and riots and avoided many of rock's most deadly clichés.

In an album that showcases Smith's natural abilities among several genres from several decades, the album's most peculiar song occurs early on, with her take on the 1985 hit "Everybody Wants to Rule the World," by Tears for Fears. Smith came across the song while in the middle of the recording of *Twelve* and was taken aback by the song's themes of the abuse of power, the misery of warfare, and man's folly against nature. Smith stated, "I was reading the news in a cafe and was really depressed. Israel had just bombed [the Lebanese village of] Qana. It made me throw my hands up and say, 'What's going on here?' And this little song comes over their sound system and I thought, 'That's exactly what's wrong with our society. We live in an imperialistic, monopoly-oriented country and planet.'"

Smith and Co. stay faithful to the song's original feel, going so far as to maintain the same tempo and reverb-drenched guitar sounds. As with the original, the feel of the song remains light while the lyrics portray a darker agenda. When Smith begins the song with "Welcome to your life, there's no turning back," she preserves the lyrical intent of stating that life is in constant motion and, as a result, people have the power to move forward and not against society—that is, by causing war or succumbing to antisocial means, which Smith displays with the lyric "Turn your back on mother nature."

What is most striking about "Everybody Wants to Rule the World" are Smith's vocals, which she delivers explicitly without any of her characteristic growl or bite that has become her trademark. The guitar solo from 2:19 to 2:49 showcases a lightness that beautifully counteracts the lyric's debilitating dark tone, which incorporates subtle note bends and flourishes that blend well with the reverb-saturated rhythm guitar.

Smith's rendition of Neil Young's "Helpless" provides a moment of reflection and clarity. Originally appearing on the 1970 Crosby, Stills, Nash, and Young album *Déjà Vu*, the song features a theme of returning to a simpler time, which proves to be a universal message that almost everyone can relate to. Smith had a bit of a history with this song, as she performed this work with Young on October 21, 1996, as a part of Young's annual Bridge School Benefit concert at the Shoreline Amphitheater in Mountain View, California.

The sparse instrumentation of guitar, bass, piano, and accordion with the lean chord progression of C Major, B Major, and A Major allows for the lyrics to take center stage and the accompaniment to perfectly showcase them. Lyrically, the use of color and shade perfectly captures the ideas that the chains of time have buried a more innocent time in one's life. Smith's delivers lines such as "Blue, blue windows behind the stars" as a way of harkening back to an earlier point in one's life, such as childhood or a simpler time in early adulthood. The result is that we are "helpless" to the idea of time and lost moments that we will never get back.

With *Twelve*'s first three offerings, Smith manipulates her voice to best suit the lyrical content of the song and perhaps the original vocal flavor of the song. The first song that Smith truly makes her own is her rendition of the Rolling Stones' classic "Gimme Shelter." First appearing on the 1969 album *Let It Bleed*, the central conceit of the song is how finite complete destruction and unfaltering love is. Each extreme begins with a singular action, with war being "just a shot away" and love being "a kiss away."

The "shelter" in question refers to a certain kind of vulnerability. When the Rolling Stones released it, this was during the Vietnam War era, a politically charged time when it seemed that the world was culturally going to meet its end. Similar to when Smith recorded the song in 2007, President George W. Bush increased the U.S. presence in Baghdad and the Al Anbar province during the Iraq War, allowing the relevance of "Gimme Shelter" to ring true to a new generation of listeners.

Smith clearly has a strong connection with the song, as she does not hold back from using the lyrics to show her disdain for war. From the onset of the song, Smith delivers the lyrics with passion and clarity, showing the provenance that she has to the material. The way that Patti delivers the line "Oh, see the fire is sweepin'" shows her disgust with war, as she snarls the word "fire" as if to reflect the fury that fire and destruction can bring.

Smith's approach to George Harrison's "Within You without You" strips away the Indian influence of the original while keeping the song's theme that life continues even if the mortal coil has ceased. The original was included on the Beatles' landmark 1967 album *Sgt. Pepper's Lonely Hearts Club Band*, and Smith beautifully articulates the psychedelic feeling of the song by utilizing a haunting, melodically static vocal delivery. Smith's reading of the line "and to see you're really only very small and life flows on within you and without you" provides a deeply humanistic context of how one's existence is small in the grand scheme yet still important to the stream of humanity. Musically, the guitar mirrors the drone of the sitar, allowing the streamlining of the song's theme.

Smith's treatment of Jefferson Airplane's "White Rabbit" is a straight-ahead exercise that feels incorporated into the sessions as a nostalgia trip. The song was originally released on the group's 1967 album *Surrealistic Pillow*. To those who came of age during this time, the summer of 1967 is known as the "summer of love," when a bridge formed combining elements of politics, war, drugs, sexual liberation, and counterculture components all under the backdrop of the Vietnam War, which was threatening to wipe out the post–World War II optimism that the United States was so desperately trying to achieve.

The introduction features Smith singing the line "Dear dear, how queer everything is today. And yesterday, things went on just as usual," using the word "queer" in an attempt to state how anomalous our society has become. The band tries to mirror the hazy feeling of the original by incorporating feedback and auxiliary guitar noises. After this, the band plays the famous introduction to the song, with a march on the snare drum signifying the entrance of an army or opposing force, accented by the bass guitar for a fuller affect.

The lyrics contain literary elements from author Lewis Carroll's *Alice in Wonderland* and *Through the Looking-Glass*, with several characters being named from the source material, including the hookah-smoking caterpillar, the White Knight, as well as the Red Queen and Dormouse. While the original exit chorus of "feed your head" might have alluded to ingesting substances and freeing your mind, Smith's take on "feed your head" feels more like she is trying to say, "Support your thoughts, nourish your desires, and nurture yourself."

Smith's decision to include Bob Dylan's "Changing of the Guards" is not the most obvious choice out of the Dylan catalog but ultimately makes sense, as the song is heavy with biblical allegory and it suits her lyrical style. It was originally recorded for Dylan's 1978 album *Street Legal,* and many felt at the time that the song was a precursor to Dylan's conversion to Christianity. However, within her voice, Patti brings out more of the apocalyptic themes of the song. Smith evokes the sense of dread and dismay that an apocalypse can bring with her delivery of the lyric "I rode past destruction in the ditches," with a slight quiver as if to ask, "How could this happen?" The soft accompaniment of the song is in direct opposition to the lyrics, as if to retain a sense of optimism within the song's gloomy feeling.

Smith's take on singer Paul Simon's "Boy in the Bubble" is lyrically the most dense, as the lyrics present in quick succession different sociopolitical issues and elements, which Smith delivers much as Simon does by utilizing a stream-of-consciousness tone. Smith's inclusion of this song on the record is a clear example of her wanting to include songs for their lyrical brevity and not because she was necessarily a fan of the original artist or composer. Speaking on NPR, Smith said, "I don't like Simon and Garfunkel music, I don't gravitate toward Paul Simon's music, but he wrote brilliant lyrics."

As the opening track to his landmark 1986 album *Graceland,* Simon concocted a song that aims to hit hard and hit fast. The beginning verse speaks about soldiers experiencing an explosion stemming from a bomb that was "wired to the radio," perhaps as a way of stating the power of sound. Outside the normal syllabic delivery that Smith is wont to use, she does not put a lot of emphasis in the emotion of the song, in an attempt to let the weight of the words ring as concise as possible. Additionally, the song speaks of duality: how the good must coexist with the bad and vice versa. In a world where technology has resulted in everything from roadside bombs to children receiving heart transplants from a baboon, children can survive by living in a bubble, and we have to accept this part of the human condition—or, as Smith has sung in agreement with Simon, "These are the days of miracle and wonder and don't cry baby, don't cry."

Smith pays tribute to Jim Morrison with her rendition to the song "Soul Kitchen," from the Doors' self-titled first album. Named after Olivia's, a small soul food restaurant at the corner of Ocean Park and Main in Los Angeles, the original version features the Doors' keyboard-ist Ray Manzarek playing a staccato rhythm on the electric organ, which creatures a jerky, funky rhythm. For Smith's rendition, the tempo is taken a lot slower, resulting in the organ sounding somber, effectively turning the song from a funky, life-affirming song to a bluesy, introspec-tive song.

The song's central theme is of desire and sexual advances, with the lyric "Let me sleep all night in your soul kitchen, warm my mind near your gentle stove," which evokes and suggests a sexual conquest. Smith delivers this line much in the same way as Morrison does by shouting it, downright demanding it from the listener. In addition to Smith's read-ing of this lyric, Smith similarly reads the song's refrain "Learn to for-get": that forgetting is a task that must be acquired, a skill that must be learned. The song's cryptic qualities play out in the lyrics "Speak in secret alphabets" and "Your fingers spin quick minarets."

Smith's inclusion of the now immortal Nirvana song "Smells like Teen Spirit" is another perfect example of her subverting expectation and making a cover her own. What is curious and most striking about Smith's interpretation is the instrumentation that she used. Originally, the song was written for the standard rock power trio of guitar, bass, and drums. For her version, Smith used bass, acoustic guitar, violin, banjo, and voice, creating a moody Appalachian folk/bluegrass feel.

The song begins with the bass playing the original distorted chords of F, Bb, Ab, Db, immediately creating a different feel from the origi-nal, as the timbre of the bass is less aggressive. The incorporation of acoustic guitar, violin, and banjo performing in polyphony creates a kind of distortion, calling back to the distortion found in the original version. To make the song truly her own, Smith recites a poem in the middle, which includes the Ginsberg-esque line "Asbestos baby bombs blasting blue." *Billboard Magazine* was especially impressed with her rendition, stating that "a daring bluegrass reworking of 'Smells Like Teen Spirit' simply startles, Smith's wizened voice transfiguring a song that's come to define youthful disaffection."

The "wizened voice" that *Billboard Magazine* speaks of is clear on the song "Midnight Rider." Written by Gregg Allman and Robert Kim Payne on the Allman Brothers Band's 1970 album *Idlewild South*, the song uses tried-and-true themes, such as running from desperation and the determination to run from demons. Speaking to NPR, Smith stated, "I just love it, I've always loved it. I reviewed it when it came out in I think 1970." This universal theme has made the song a popular standard among musicians of several genres and periods, with rock singer Joe Cocker, reggae singer Paul Davidson, country singer Waylon Jennings, and doo-wop singers the Drifters adding their spins to the original song.

In the original song, the central hook of "I've got one more silver dollar, but I'm not gonna let 'em catch me" is sung by Gregg Allman and the rest of the band, creating a feel that they are outlaws on the run. In Smith's rendition, she sings it with such confidence that it evokes the feeling that she is reflecting on a journey that has taken her around and back and that staying on this journey is necessary before life ultimately gets you.

Twelve ends with Smith's interpretation of the Stevie Wonder song "Pastime Paradise." Originally released on Wonder's hit 1976 album *Songs in the Key of Life*, the song has been covered by several artists throughout the years, including Latin jazz musician Ray Barretto and soul band Sunlightsquare. The most notable version was done by rapper Coolio in 1995, which, while not a complete cover, sampled the main instrumental riff and the chorus for his hit song "Gangsta's Paradise."

One can see why the song would be a great fit for a cover, as its themes are open to interpretation. One interpretation is the idea of living your life in the moment rather than spending one's life dealing with the scars of our past and the anxieties of our future. As a result, every moment that you are living is being robbed of the enjoyment that you could be having. Smith perfectly reflects this during the choruses, where her weathered delivery of the central lyric "They've been spending most their lives living in a future paradise" is wrought with emotion, leaving the listener to decide whether or not she is dealing with the scars of the past or the anxieties of her future.

Another interpretation of the song is that it is a meditation on how modern society has so many negative connotations and so many means to deliver such connotations. Smith's sorrowful breath sets forth a menu of social problems, from race to religion to economic illusions, by singing vague phrases such as "race relations" and "exploitation" without any further explanation. However, Wonder's final statement defines the actual message of the song: "Let's start living our lives, living for the future paradise," as opposed to living in the unhappy past or the illusory future to escape present social issues.

Although the set of songs that Smith decided to record on *Twelve* showcases her vocal range and tastes, she excluded several songs that she recorded, thinking that they did not showcase her voice well enough. Included on this list was Lou Reed's "Perfect Day," REM's "Everybody Hurts," the Dead Boy's "Sonic Reducer," and the Decemberists' "Here I Dreamt I Was an Architect." Smith's rendition of REM's "Everybody Hurts" keeps intact the original, with its steadfast tempo and dreary-eyed pace. Swapping out the guitar riff for a Fender Rhoades sound, the constant D major to G major riff that made the song so iconic is made all the more enriching with the reverb sound that the Fender Rhodes has.

Whether Smith knew it or not, the members of REM planned to include her in their original recording of the song. In an interview, REM's bassist Mike Mills stated that he wanted Smith to sing on the song when it was released on the album *Automatic for the People*, but the band was not able to secure her for the session, as "she was busy with her family, and she was working, and being a mother and a wife." REM singer Michael Stipe said that he had originally envisioned the song as a duet between the two of them.

Twelve entered the *Billboard Magazine*'s Top 200 charts at 60, with eleven thousand copies sold in its first week. While the aim of the album was to showcase Smith's voice, many reviewers were quick to point out that the covers were missing the usual Smith fire that they had come to expect. Joshua Klein from *Pitchfork Media* stated, "Smith's shockingly conservative eleventh studio album . . . comprises twelve mostly predictable covers and seems suspiciously timed to take advantage of Smith's recent induction into the Rock and Roll Hall of Fame (after seven straight years of being nominated)."

Perhaps the most scathing review came from Jimmy Newlin from *Slant Magazine*: "The selection of songs on Patti Smith's covers album *Twelve* is so obvious and stale that 'Weird Al' Yankovic has already covered many of them (Nirvana's 'Smells Like Teen Spirit' and Stevie Wonder's 'Pastime Paradise' by way of Coolio)." While not fully giving the album a positive review, Tom Useted from *Popmatters* stated that while the album is not fully successful, Smith's choice of cover songs is something to commend: "Even if the sources of much of Smith's material are yawn-inducing, it's pretty difficult to find fault with some of her picks." Furthermore, Useted praised Smith choice of covering Dylan's "Changing of the Guards" instead of a more popular Dylan song that she could easily have done.

As part of the promotional pull for *Twelve*, Smith and the band performed a series of concerts in New York City entitled "The Bowery Sessions." Taking place on April 24, 2007, at the Bowery Ballroom, fans were given the opportunity to receive a ticket to one of three thirty-minute performances upon the purchase of *Twelve*. Each concert featured Smith and some of the band performing a half hour of songs, as well as answering questions from the audience and reading some poetry. Patti Smith spent the remainder of 2007 on the road, visiting locales all over Europe and America playing high-profile gigs, culminating with a three-night stint at the Bowery Ballroom from December 29 to December 31.

The subsequent year saw the release of *Patti Smith: Dream of Life*, a documentary film nearly thirteen years in the making. Directed by Steven Sebring, the project began in 1995 when Sebring was selected by Smith to photograph her for *Spin Magazine*. The two struck up a conversation, eventually spending the day together drinking coffee. Smith was reluctant to be the subject of a documentary, believing at that point in her career she had not accomplished enough. Speaking to Neal Conan of NPR, Smith said, "I wasn't so certain that I had achieved enough to merit a documentary, but Steven offered to shoot our comings and goings on his own. He was not invasive. He was like a brother shooting us." *Dream of Life* was shown at both the Berlin International Film Festival and the Sundance Film Festival, winning the award of "Excellence in Cinematography Award: Documentary" at Sundance. The documentary eventually aired on PBS on December 30, 2009, on Patti's sixty-third birthday.

The year 2010 would be Smith's most high-profile year in recent memory. Smith would bring her career full circle by revisiting her early years, not through music, but through prose. Patti sowed the seeds of this project years prior . . . with a promise.

10

"JUST PATTI"

2010–Present

Nostalgia can be a tricky phenomenon. Depending on whose hands it's in, nostalgia can be a blessing or a curse. On one hand, it can be a beautiful memory of times past, something that we can escape to when the going gets tough. On the other, nostalgia can be a cruel reminder of a sour time that should be forgotten. How one remembers the events of one's life is, at its core, a large undertaking that an individual must constantly confront as humanity. Author Neil Gaiman in his 1994 graphic novel *The Tragical Comedy or Comical Tragedy of Mr. Punch* speaks of nostalgia and memory as "neither straight or safe, and we travel down it at our risk." For Patti, the trip down memory lane brought unparalleled success.

The year 2010 began with the publication of Patti's book *Just Kids*, a memoir documenting her early years in New York City and her relationship with Mapplethorpe. The seeds of *Just Kids* were sown on Mapplethorpe's deathbed. Lying beside him as he clung to life, Patti asked Robert what he wanted her to do, how she could continue working with him. Mapplethorpe responded with "Well, you tell our story. You're the only would that could tell it." *Just Kids* seamlessly juxtaposes the romantic notion of insouciant youth with a gripping story of Smith's growth as an artist. In her review for the *Washington Post*, critic Elizabeth Hand stated that *Just Kids* is "one of the best books ever written on becoming an artist."

Just Kids was met with near universal acclaim and brought Smith back to the front lines of commercial and critical recognition. *Just Kids* would ultimately win the 2010 National Book Award for Nonfiction, grace the best-of lists for the *Los Angeles Times* and *New York Times*, and receive numerous other accolades.

The high-profile success of *Just Kids* kept Smith in constant demand, with a new generation of people discovering or rediscovering Patti's work. On May 17, 2010, Smith was invited to deliver the commencement address for the graduating class of the Pratt Institute at New York's famed Radio City Music Hall. In true self-deprecating, Carson-esque style, Smith opened with a joke that easily broke the ice, stating that her generation lacked good dental care and that the dentists of her generation were former army dentists who still thought of the dentist's office as a "battle ground." Smith went on to say that the fire that is inside all of us, that urge to create that makes you pace around at night, should be your focus, not pacing around because "you need a damn root canal."

Smith continued her speech, showing lovely vulnerability and sweetness, a purity of intent from one soul to thousands. During the address, Smith compared herself to Pinocchio, as they both went out in the world with a vision, good intentions, and dreams within their reach. Both made mistakes; both tried and failed—but they kept at it, as they both had that flame inside them that could not be extinguished, no matter what. Smith sweetly ended her address by simply stating, "Be happy, take care of your teeth, always let your conscience be your guide."

The whimsical New York Patti spoke of in *Just Kids* reminded the reader of a time in New York where one could afford to be a broke artist, clinging to life in the name of art. However, the changing economic landscape of New York City fed into Smith's beliefs that New York City was no longer the go-to place for artists to follow and develop their craft. In conversation with author Jonathan Lethem at Cooper Union in New York, a question-and-answer segment showed with pinpoint accuracy how Smith viewed New York City in the modern era. A woman in the audience asked whether it was possible for a young artist to move to New York City and make it as an artist. Smith responded with, "New York has closed itself off to the young and the struggling. But there are other cities. Detroit. Poughkeepsie. New York City has been taken away from you. So my advice is: Find a new city." The bleak indictment of New York City shocked many but showed that Patti was still willing to take chances and speak her mind to whoever asked.

The post–*Just Kids* acclaim continued for Smith, even on an international level. On August 30, 2011, Smith was awarded Sweden's "Polar Music Prize," the nation's highest music honor. Before a glitzy Stockholm crowd, Smith took the stage and, in true punk rock style, chose to use the spotlight as an opportunity to call out and speak her mind. While she did mention that she was humbled in receiving the award, Smith quickly turned her attention toward the atrocities in East Africa, where famine continues to be a big problem. Smith asked audience members that they "turn their hearts, minds and resources" to the disaster.

Smith also proved in 2011 that she could still be adventurous and unexpected. In an interesting turn for Smith, Patti guest starred on the popular NBC police procedural *Law and Order: Criminal Intent*, where she played the character "Cleo Alexander," a professor of mythology brought in to help the team solve the apparent murder of an actor who was performing in a Broadway play based on the Greek story of Icarus. Smith herself was a fan of *Law and Order* and often watched episodes while on the road. Smith was so much of a fan of the show—in particular, the character Detective Robert Goren, played by actor Vincent D'Onofrio—that her desire to watch the show was the impetus for her purchasing a television. Smith later stated, "When I was offered a small part, I accepted for the great pleasure of interacting with my favorite detective."

The success of *Just Kids*, if the stars are properly aligned, will provide Smith with an additional medium to conquer. On August 15, 2011, *Deadline Hollywood* reported that Smith would be adapting *Just Kids* into a movie. Cowriting the screenplay with screenwriter John Logan— most known for penning the Academy Award–winning movie *Hugo* and the Tony Award–winning play *Red*—Smith voiced her enthusiasm for actors Kristen Stewart and Robert Pattinson to portray herself and Mapplethorpe in the movie. Stewart and Pattinson are most famous for costarring together in the popular *Twilight* movies and themselves dating in the past. Smith stated before a private concert at KCRW in Los Angeles, "I remember the very first time I saw Kristen Stewart and Rob Pattinson together, when they were younger, and I thought, 'Those two kids could have easily played us when they were first starting.'" Smith also expressed that, as Mapplethorpe and she were unknown at the time, whoever play them in the movie should be equally unknown. Smith said, "Robert and I were very young. We were twenty. We were unknowns, and I think it should be unknowns in the film, and young."

When it came time to begin working on material for her latest album, Smith called on her literature roots for inspiration. Entitled *Banga*, the title refers to the book *The Master and Margarita*, the postmodern Russian comedy by author Mikhail Bulgakov. The book tells the story of the Master, an author who has written a novel about a meeting between Pontius Pilate and Yeshua Ha-Notsri. The novel speaks about the duality between good and evil, right and wrong, and the courage that one must muster to challenge one's government.

The character "Banga" was the Master's dog, a faithful servant that loved and respected his owner as the most powerful man in the world, the ruler of all men, thanks to whom the dog considered himself a privileged, lofty, and special being. *Banga* showcases Smith as a contemporary den mother, quick to soothe, salute, or pay tribute to anyone she sees worthy. On this list includes Mapplethorpe, actress Maria Schneider, filmmaker Andrei Tarkovsky, novelist Nikoli Gogol, actor Johnny Depp, New World explorer Amerigo Vespucci, and the survivors of the Japanese tsunami.

The impetus of *Banga* came from a message from Jean-Luc Goddard, the legendary French New Wave filmmaker known for such films as *Breathless*, *Band of Outsiders*, and *My Life to Live*. Godard called Smith and instructed her with the following statement: "one good American." With this cryptic message, Smith began to compose the material that would eventually make its way on *Banga* while being on a ship at sea filming a cameo in Godard's 2010 film *Socialism*. Having never been at sea before, the experience provided Smith time to contemplate and think of sea exploration and the feelings that come from being at sea.

Banga is her first album of new material since 2004's *Trampin* and her first album since 2007's *Twelve*. Smith had to think about who she was during this time and what it meant to provide art to people. Speaking to *Rolling Stone*, Smith stated, "It was something I had to wrestle with: Who am I now and what can I give to the people?" Smith said. "To give people a new record, I have to evolve, have new things to share. I needed those years of traipsing around." The success of *Just Kids* also proved to be influential in its own way as well. Speaking to WNYC, Smith mentioned, "I think the travels and experiences I had informed the songs but also the welcoming from the people all over the world for the book, which I never dreamed, I didn't anticipate that."

Banga begins with "Amerigo," which examines Smith's thoughts on sea exploration and the vast beyond that the open sea promises. Using famous Italian explorer and cartographer Amerigo Vespucci as her eyes, Smith describes what he sees upon discovering the New World. Smith outlines how Vespucci sees the indigenous people living in their own liberty and how they "had neither King nor Lord." Smith paints Vespucci more as a character as opposed to a living, breathing person and offers a sensitive take on how Vespucci views the inhabitants of this so-called new, undiscovered continent. Smith ruminates on the colonial impulse to immediately baptize with the line "We placed baptismal fonts and an infinite number were baptized," which is sung at the beginning and subsequently returned to toward the end of the song, where she speaks of everyone dancing naked while being "baptized in the rain of the New World."

"Amerigo" shows Smith and the band at their most instrumentally lush, with a string section adding long, sustained notes that augment Smith's soft voice. The way that the song builds is noteworthy, as it begins with Daugherty playing a single D on the piano, with Smith quickly following with a spoken-word excerpt. Subsequent, the rhythm guitar and drums join Patti, tailed by the string section, painting a picture that this song, along with the album itself, will build off the musical components rather than administer everything at once.

The album's single "April Fool" was inspired by noted Russian writer Nikolai Gogol, whose literary output ran the gamut of literary and social themes much in the way that Patti's music does. Gogol was born from the natural school of Russian literary realism, which thought that literature should mirror reality. Alongside this idea, Gogol peppered his work with surrealistic tendencies and political satire, much to the chagrin of the Russian empire. Patti dedicated "April Fool" to her friend Milos, who introduced her to the works of Gogol.

Cleverly released as the album's single on April 1, 2012, the song may very well be Smith at her most radio friendly since she recorded *Dream of Life*. Benefiting from a straightforward tempo and the upbeat vibe of Daugherty's electric organ, Smith spreads the lyrics with a soft palette, adding a romantic tone to the song's lighthearted, carefree spirit. This is augmented by the light guitar ornamentations from Tom Verlaine, whose reverb/delayed drenched tone fits perfectly within the song's structure.

Lyrically, "April Fool" evokes the idea of two people who have not a care in the world and wish only to live their lives to the fullest. This bohemian ideal is in full force as Patti sings, "Race through alleyways in our tattered coats," conjuring a spirit of Rimbaud or Oscar Wilde running free in a European city. Critic David Marren in his review for *Louder Than War* goes a step further and states that the song "sounds like an aural interpretation of her *Just Kids* biography and you can almost visualize her and Robert Mapplethorpe taking off on their bikes to embrace their young adventures to change the world."

Smith switches gears with "Fuji-san," a song dedicated to the Japanese people who inhabited the Oshika Peninsula and the horror they experienced on March 11, 2011, when the Tohoku earthquake and tsunami took the lives of more than fifteen thousand people. The total estimated economic impact was more than $235 billion, making it the costliest natural disaster in world history. Smith wrote in the liner notes to *Banga* that the song was "a call of prayer to the great mountain—for a protective cloak of love."

Taking its name from Mount Fuji, the song begins with a monk's prayer, highlighting the song's overall religious dedication to the Japanese people. The genesis of the song began backstage at Carnegie Hall during the annual Tibet House benefit concert. Kaye, who was messing around on his acoustic guitar, began playing the riff of the song. Smith immediately came over to him to ask what he was playing, not realizing what it was. Soon after, the band met up at its practice space and began to build on what would eventually become "Fuji-san."

For a song that feels like it could have been a part of REM's early catalog, with its jangly guitar tone and lo-fi qualities, "Fuji-san" begins on a rather ominous note: with guitar feedback and powerful, sparse drums stewing while Smith calls on Mount Fuji by asking, "Oh, mountain of our eyes, what do you see?" The religious undercurrent evokes the picture of monks praying to Mount Fuji when Smith sings "Mortal soldiers clear the path, shake the omen tree Oh, mountain of our eyes, oh plea, Oh, hear our plea." The ominous tone quickly fades as the introduction of Kaye's guitar riff, with its constantly playing on the A string adds a powerful pedal point, a musical constant that provides the song with a natural musical arc.

Banga shifts with a pair of back-to-back elegies. The first is "This Is the Girl," written in memory of singer Amy Winehouse, who died on July 23, 2011, at the age of twenty-seven due to alcohol poisoning. On writing the song and observing the death of Winehouse, Smith stated in *Billboard Magazine*, "I felt very saddened by that, I thought she was extremely gifted. I loved her voice. I thought it was a very important voice, very authentic, and I just wrote a little poem for her when she died." While recording *Banga*, bassist Tony Shanahan came to Patti with another piece of music. Already fearing that the album had too many songs, Smith initially eschewed the song. However, after listening to the piece of music that Tony bought in, Smith realized that her poem to Winehouse and his music matched perfectly.

"This Is the Girl" is a near pitch-perfect representation of 1950s and 1960s R&B/soul girl group charisma. Should the lyrics not have been about the death of an artist who passed so soon, one could close one's eyes and see a young couple parked upon a hilltop looking out at their future. With its gentle, waltz feel along soft background vocal lines, Smith executes a song that would be close to Winehouse's heart. Smith evokes her image by singing about her heavily made-up eyes and how it was perhaps a mask to hide her sadness ("Just a dark smear masking the eyes, spirited away hurrying inside"). Smith could easily risk sentimentality with such a song, but she easily avoids such a tone. Smith sings, "This is the girl who crossed the line," not condemning her for her actions, simply pointing out that a fellow artist lost her way.

"Maria" is partially in tribute to the late actress Maria Schneider, most known for the controversial movie *Last Tango in Paris*, which she starred in alongside actor Marlon Brando. Schneider toured with Smith in 1976, and the loss of Schneider drew Smith back to that time. Speaking to WNYC, Smith stated, "The loss of her really threw me back to that period with such clarity and the words just tumbled out. It's not really just about Maria, but Robert is in it, all of us are in it. The '70s is in it." Smith also stated that among all the tracks on *Banga*, "Maria" is the most nostalgic and the most personal.

"Maria" is also a well-placed emotional high point, one where the album's sense of exploration and observation reaches a logical extreme by taking on the world from the view of a departed, worldly citizen. The song mirrors the waltz feel from "This Is the Girl" but replaces the girl group hipness with a more somber, reflective tone, augmented with ease by Daugherty's weightless performance and timbre. The nostalgia that permeates from "Maria" is clearly detailed in the lyric "I knew you when we were young, I knew you, now you're gone," using Schneider's death as a way of eulogizing not only her but a simpler time. Smith perhaps also comments on herself amid this with the lyric "Wild wild hair, sad sad eyes. White shirt, black tie—you were mine." While this may very well be a description of Schneider, the "wild wild hair" and "white shirt" easily evoke a picture of Smith from the cover of *Horses*.

The album's title track is conveniently placed in the middle of the album and acts as palette cleanser, like the opening of a second act of a play or the second movement of a symphonic work. With the first half of the album concentrating on everything from colonial baptism to the deaths of two artists, the near absurdist, punk-searing sensibility that "Banga" provides completely adds a much-needed breath of fresh air to the album. The song takes its title from a character in *The Master and the Margarita*. Serving as Pontius Pilate's faithful dog, Banga was a loyal friend and never left his side, even waiting with his master for two thousand years outside the territory of Heaven so that his master could speak with Jesus Christ. In a promotion video that went along with the release of *Banga*, Smith stated, "Any dog that waited patiently for 2,000 years deserved a song."

Smith begins the lyrics by stating how loyal a dog is, as loyalty itself is "in the heart of a dog." Smith contextualizes the trust that a dog gives by stating that man would never trust his life to any other animal, particularly an animal that is temperamental, such as a frog, upon whose back you would not want to "set all your eggs." The absurd moments come courtesy of dog barks in the background vocals and Smith emulating the guitar drones, like a pest mocking it. In an interview with Smith for *The Telegraph*, Craig McLean equates some of the guitar noises to that of a "canine howl." The "howl" in question came courtesy of actor Johnny Depp, who Smith insisted is "a really great musician," so much so that the opening of *Banga* is just "Johnny on guitar, Johnny on drums, Johnny on bass—and my vocal." The song culminates in a sudden stop and resulting feedback fade-out, with Smith beautifully enunciating "explode," daring the listener to forcefully respond.

"Mosaic" shows how far-reaching Smith's influences are, as the song was inspired by the twelfth-century Persian Mevlana Jalaluddin Rumi and the character Katniss Everdeen of the popular literary trilogy *The Hunger Games*. Speaking to Mary M. Lane of the *Wall Street Journal*, Smith stated, "I saw the film—I didn't read the books—and I was quite taken by her. When I was younger, I would have loved to play a part [in the film]. There's a bit of Joan of Arc in her; she's going to be the salvation of her people. Her weapon of choice, the bow and arrow, is very romantic like Artemis, so that seeped into the song."

Musically, the song calls on timbres found in Anatolian rock, a fusion of Turkish folk and rock and roll. The acoustic guitar keeps an even strumming pattern while auxiliary guitars perform slight, reverb-fueled tones, sounding like a sitar. Joined with Smith's deep vocal delivery of neutral-syllabic wails, the music sounds as if it were meant for a religious ceremony. At the beginning of the song, Smith brings us to the Turkish city of Konya, where the shrine of Rumi is housed. Smith evokes the spirit of Rumi when she sings, "In the ring of fire, in the sleep of peace, nothing stops desire for the human beat," which mirrors the Rumi's conviction that the human spirit, whether being threatened or no longer living, is something to be desired and is something that people need.

Smith continues to showcases how adept she is at atmosphere with "Tarkovsky (the Second Stop Is Jupiter)," a tribute to Russian filmmaker and director Andrei Tarkovsky. Tarkovsky made a career out of utilizing experimental techniques, such as extended takes, disjointed narrative structures, and the use of metaphysical themes. Smith tries to reflect such themes by incorporating improvisation, multilayers of instruments, and brief narrative threads that she carefully ties together. The atmosphere that she creates, though, is all her own and sounds as if she is narrating a neonoir film or perhaps performing in a New York café in the 1950s alongside her Beat brethren. Beginning with a xylophone that outlines an F# minor chord, the band slowly creeps into the song with two guitars, one improving and the other performing tremolo-drenched chords, resulting in a sonic duel. The drums slowly perform accents on the cymbals before segueing into a jazz riff by keeping the beat on the ride cymbal.

The lyrics of the song have their genesis in a poem that she wrote titled "The Boy, the Beast and the Butterfly," which she performed on

January 1, 2010, as part of her annual performance at the St. Marks Church Poetry Project Marathon in New York City. Lyrically, the song plays out like a Tarkovsky "Greatest Hits" collection. The line "Black moon shines on a lake, white as a hand in the dark" and "Come along, sweet lad, fog rises from the ground" seem inspired by scenes from the Tartovsky's first film *Ivan's Childhood*, which tells the story of a young boy named Ivan and his life during World War II. The line "The telegraph poles are crosses on the line, rusted pins, not enough saviors to hang" references Tartovsky's 1979 film *Stalker*, and the mysterious and dangerous are known as the "Zone" that the titular "stalker" uses in an attempt to fulfill someone's desires.

"Nine" was written as a present to Depp, whom she had met a few years prior backstage at the Orpheum Theater in Los Angeles. Partly inspired by Depp's birthday—June 9—Smith wrote the song in Puerto Rico while Depp was filming the movie *The Rum Diary*. "Nine" gently blends two ensemble palettes effortlessly, with the rhythm section playing a gentle folk style and with the superb Tom Verlaine displaying a more rock-tinged style. Lyrically, Smith speaks of an individual who has the aura of luck around him but is "more vagabond than king." Assuming that this person in question is Depp, Smith speaks of him as being "another kind of strange," but Smith's vocal delivery shows nothing but sincerity and heart in speaking of her friend the vagabond.

The imagery of being out at sea and in Godard's viewfinder makes its way on the track "Seneca." Written as a lullaby for her godson Seneca Sebring, the gentle waltz uses the sea as a metaphor for life and as an instrument to find one's purpose in life. Smith tenderly decries "run, run my little one, run out to sea" as a way of telling her godson to not be afraid of the life that he is about to lead but to be brave and journey out to the sea of life. Smith's vocal delivery, while trying to voice a lullaby, comes off solemn and harrowed. In her review for *The Guardian*, author Kitty Empire states—when Smith sings, "Oh crown of wind, two royal leopards run with him"—that "out of context it might read like sophomoric poeticism, but like every song Smith sings it comes to the ear like a spell."

That spell-like feel is partially due to the lyrics but also due to the subtle instrumentation of the song. The acoustic guitar carefully follows that waltz rhythm by never deviating outside the "1–2–3" "1–2–3" feel, which allows the other instruments to carefully shine through the arrangement. The interesting juxtaposition of steel guitar, accordion, bass, and violin lends itself to the spell-like feel by performing long, dronelike countermelodies, putting the listener in a trance. At different points of the song, instruments trade off in doubling Smith's vocal line, creating an ethereal effect to the song.

"Constantine's Dream" is a dense meditation on the competing vocations of art and faith via the lives of Francis of Assisi, Emperor Constantine, painter Piero della Francesca, and Christopher Columbus. The title specifically refers to Constantine the Great, the Roman emperor who ruled over the empire from 306 to 337. Most notable during his reign was the many protocols and reforms that he began that ultimately strengthened his administration. One such reform was the "Edict of Milan," a proclamation that permanently established religious toleration for Christianity within the Roman Empire. This decree assured Christians of legal rights (including the right to organize churches), and it directed the prompt return of confiscated property to Christians. Previous edicts of toleration had been as short-lived as the regimes that sanctioned them, but this time the edict effectively established religious toleration.

A dense, apocalyptic vision of environmental destruction with a "Kashmir"-like vamp, over a shifting series of musical settings, "Constantine's Dream" revisits themes introduced by "Amerigo." In a dreamlike visit to an Italian church, the singer is torn between a direct experience of nature, represented by St. Francis, and beauty's representation in the form of art. The song is the second track about voyages to America, on which Smith tackles the very nature of art—and the art of nature.

Smith begins "Constantine's Dream" by placing herself in the Italian city of Arezzo, recounting a dream that she had about St. Francis, kneeling and praying for all of humankind. While Smith is recounting this dream, a classical guitar arpeggiates a chord, painting a beautiful picture of Smith standing in Tuscany, contemplating the role of art and the role of the artist. While further recounting a visit to St. Francis's basilica, a narrator of sorts recites St. Francis's prayer in Italian. The prayer acts as a meditation for all who desire peace. St. Francis recognized that he and all who recite this prayer would run up against people and circumstances that will be threatening. The group slowly increases the dynamics of the music as Smith's decrees about art becoming all the more impassioned, as the final lyric "And the dream of the troubled King dissolved into light" caps off a fury of improvisation that slowly fades into the musical horizon.

Banga ends with a cover of the Neil Young song "After the Gold Rush," which features Smith's children Jackson and Jesse. Smith stated that she wanted to end the album with "some semblance of light or dawn or a bit of hope" after the concentrated rage of "Constantine's Dream." "I was in a café and I happened to hear 'After the Gold Rush' and I listened to the lyrics and a lot of the lyrics fit well, the words, the references fit well with 'Constantine's Dream' and it offered all the things I wanted to present."

The song's three stanzas could easily be viewed as a discussion about Earth in the past, present, and future. The first stanza speaks of "knights in armor" and "peasants singing," bringing to mind a clear time of the past, perhaps the medieval era on account of the knights. Earth as represented in the first verse is rather untouched, with "the fanfare floating on the breeze." Earth of the second verse is a war-torn place, with the main character of the song wishing what he had been told by a friend were a lie, "hoping it was a lie."

The last verse tells about the final days of Earth, when it has been destroyed by humans and we need to find a new home in the universe, but not everybody can make the journey—hence, "there were children cryin' and colors flyin' all around the chosen ones." "After the Gold Rush" ends with a choir of children singing, which included bassist Tony Shanahan's nephew and a few of his classmates. The inclusion of a children's choir as the last moments that the listener hears leaves the lingering sense of purity and hope.

Critics welcomed *Banga* with open arms after what many saw as a critical misstep with Smith's previous effort, *Twelve*. Kitty Empire of *The Guardian* states that *Banga* is the "most satisfying of her latter-day career." Empire is also quick to point out that Smith is far too reserved when a major theme of the album is destruction. Empire voices this in her review by stating, "This record, whose central theme is destruction, might be playing too nice. The single, 'April Fool,' bobs along perkily, as accessible as Smith has ever been."

Evelyn McDonnell of the *Los Angeles Times* points out that Smith took a sizable risk with the material on *Banga*, stating after the success of *Just Kids* that she could have easily taken the road that many of her contemporaries have done and recorded an album of standards or covers (which she noted that Smith already did on *Twelve*). McDonnell further states that when an artist decides to take a risk, it does not always work, but Smith in taking a risk has reinvigorated her music. Few showed disinterest in Smith's return, with John Aizlewood of the *London Evening Standard* providing perhaps the most scathing review of *Banga*. Aizlewood parses that most of the album sounds "bereft of spirit and distracted," with her version of "After the Gold Rush" as "the exact moment Patti Smith ran out of ideas."

Smith and the band spent the remainder of the summer performing all throughout Europe before coming stateside in September for a number of West Coast dates before heading back to Europe. The success of *Just Kids* continued to make Smith a hot commodity in the literary community. In December 2012, Smith announced that she would be penning a sequel of sorts to *Just Kids*. The untitled book will continue with the tone that Smith created with *Just Kids*, but it will shift more to family, her relationship with Fred, and her music. Smith jokingly mentioned that while her lifestyle is not of the grand sex, drugs, and rock-'n'-roll schema that many of her contemporaries lived, her refraining from such situations had perhaps warranted her a better story to tell. Smith states, "I think I have maybe a better story. Through rock 'n' roll I traveled the world, worked with my late brother [Todd] and, best of all, that's how I met Fred. It changed my life in many unexpected ways, so I have my story to tell."

The following year saw Hollywood aiming to tell the story of CBGB. Director/writer Randall Miller alongside cowriter Jody Savin released the movie *CBGB*, a fictionalized movie regarding the early years of the club and the musicians and bands that came through its halls. Sporting a cast that included Alan Rickman as Hilly Kristal, Malin Akerman as Debbie Harry, and Taylor Hawkins as Iggy Pop, Smith had reservations about the production of the movie. On the movie, Smith stated, "Don't understand why anybody wants to play a living person. But, I don't . . . you know, to me, we lived through that period. It seems ridiculous to be filming it."

For the movie, Smith was portrayed by Mickey Sumner, daughter of singer-bassist Sting, whose band the Police received its breakthrough in North America by performing at the famed club. Miller stated that Smith was particularly hard to cast, as her look and style had to be perfect. Sumner herself was a big Smith fan and went so far to ask Smith for permission to play her in the movie. The movie was met with negative reviews, with Judy Berman of Flavorwire.com stating, "The female characters come off especially terribly; Miller and Savin seem to have confused Patti Smith's persona with [singer] Lydia Lunch's."

On October 27, 2013, Smith and the New York music scene in general were dealt a serious blow when Lou Reed passed away after a long bout with liver disease. Smith received news of his passing while strolling the beaches of a hurricane-beaten Rockaway Beach via text message from her daughter. Smith had run into Reed and his wife, performance artist Laurie Anderson, and Smith could not help be see the weariness in her eyes. Upon saying good-bye, Smith stated that Reed's "dark eyes seemed to contain an infinite and benevolent sadness." The passing of Reed came as another New York life lost, another one that we won't get back.

For her sixty-seventh birthday, Smith performed at Webster Hall in New York City and took time out toward the end of her set to praise infamous whistleblower Edward Snowden and newly liberated Russian punk rockers Pussy Riot. Smith praised Pussy Riot stars Nadezhda Tolokonnikova and Maria Alekhina, who were freed from a Russian work camp on December 23, 2013, after serving nearly two years on hooliganism charges for staging a controversial church protest against Russian leader Vladimir Putin. Smith upon speaking to New York's *Newsday* voiced her concern for the two women, who at the time of the interview were still incarcerated. Speaking to author Steve Knopper, Smith stated, "their people [Pussy Riot's] contact me and I hear how they're faring, but one can't ever be sure about these things till they happen. I'll be overjoyed to see them out. They have suffered long enough and I get concerned about their physical health."

Patti stated how happy she was that the punks "continue to use their voice, because it's very dangerous for them to do so," and she told the audience, "Do not underestimate the danger those girls face by speaking their mind." She continued, "Edward Snowden, Pussy Riot, these people speak for us all, all of us who are no longer numb, all of us who are no longer dumb." In a new song, she even changed the lyrics to take a shot at the U.S. National Security Agency, singing, "All of our phone numbers, all of our personal business, the business of our government, Edward let it snow, Edward let it snow," referring to Snowden's efforts to expose the extent of surveillance operations that the United States was implementing.

On March 28, 2014, director Darren Aronofsky released the movie *Noah*, detailing the life of the biblical hero and the construction of his ark. For the film's soundtrack, Patti contributed "Mercy Is," a song featuring her with the famed string ensemble the Kronos Quartet. The genesis of the project came one year during the Venice Film Festival where Darren was telling Patti about an idea he had about a cinematic telling of Noah. Speaking to Mary Anne Hobbs from *BBC Radio*, Smith stated how Darren mentioned that he "needed a lullaby for the movie that Noah would sing to a young child." Smith further stated that she has a secret affinity for writing lullabies and she asked Darren outright to have a hand in writing it.

The recording process for the song did prove to have its share of challenges. After a lifetime of performing with her group, Smith found the lack of a clearly defined rhythm section difficult: "I record live with my own band all of the time but that's with a bass and drums and you always know where you are even if you're improvising but it was an unusual experience for me to record life with a string quartet. It was beautiful but I have to say challenging so we all had to play 'til we were all completely relaxed and of one mind." In his review of the soundtrack for *Allmusic.com*, critic Thom Jurek mentioned that Smith's lyrics and vocals feature "a gorgeous, nearly Anglo-Celtic melody."

With her seventieth year approaching, Patti continues to expand her creative output with book projects, touring, and new music on the horizon. What is certain is that Patti's message of hard work and staying true to yourself blends any distinction that she is of any generation; rather, she is generational and timeless. Patti may be the "godmother of punk," but a more fitting title is "America's punk rock rhapsodist."

FURTHER READING

36doggy. "Patti Smith Group-SNL-Gloria." https://www.youtube.com/watch?v=yy9fs3cndrQ.

"500 Greatest Albums of All Time." *Rolling Stone*. http://www.rollingstone.com/music/lists/500-greatest-albums-of-all-time-20120531/patti-smith-horses-20120524.

"500 Greatest Songs of All Time." *Rolling Stone*. http://www.rollingstone.com/music/lists/the-500-greatest-songs-of-all-time-20110407/patti-smith-group-dancing-barefoot-20110526.

Adams, Sam. "Charles Burns: Interview." *The AV Club*. http://www.avclub.com/article/charles-burns-47913.

Aizlewood, John. "CDs of the Week." *London Evening Standard*. http://www.standard.co.uk/goingout/music/cds-of-the-week-7394361.html.

Bangs, Lester. "Stagger Lee Was a Woman." *Creem*. February 1976. http://www.oceanstar.com/patti/crit/76bangs.htm.

Berman, Judy. "'CBGB' the Movie Somehow Manages to Make Punk Rock Boring." October 11, 2013. http://flavorwire.com/419411/cbgb-the-movie-somehow-manages-to-make-punk-rock-boring.

"The Best Live Acts Now." *Rolling Stone*. August 15, 2013: 44.

Bockris, Victor, and Roberta Bayley. *Patti Smith: An Unauthorized Biography*. New York: Simon & Schuster, 1999: 20, 22, 44, 45.

Boilen, Bob. "All Songs Considered: Guest DJ Patti Smith." National Public Radio. June 19, 2012. http://www.npr.org/2012/06/19/155291456/guest-dj-patti-smith.

Bosso, Joe. "Production Legend Jack Douglas on 18 Career-Defining Records." *MusicRadar.com*. December 19, 2012. Web. http://www.musicradar.com/us/news/guitars/production-legend-jack-douglas-on-18-career-defining-records-568681/1

Brazier, Chris. "Patti's Easter Rising." *Melody Maker*. March 4, 1978. http://www.oceanstar.com/patti/crit/7803melo.htm.

Browne, David. "Patti Smith: Gung Ho." *Entertainment Weekly*. March 27, 2000. http://www.ew.com/ew/article/0,,64602,00.html.

———. "Smith & Lessons." *Entertainment Weekly*. June 12, 1996. http://www.oceanstar.com/patti/crit/gaentwk.htm.

Brownstein, Carrie. "Five Women Every Man Should Listen To." *Esquire*. April 19, 2011. http://www.esquire.com/features/music/best-female-singers-0511.

Callwood, Brett. *MC5: Sonically Speaking: A Tale of Revolution and Rock 'n' Roll*. Detroit, MI: Wayne State University Press, 2010: 13, 169, 180.

Carson, Tom. "A Real Drip—Patti Smith: Under the Double Ego." *Rolling Stone*. June 28, 1979. http://www.oceanstar.com/patti/crit/rswave.htm.

Cassata, Mary Anne. "The Ongoing Dream, as of 1988." *The Music Paper*. October 1988. http://www.oceanstar.com/patti/intervus/881000ms.htm.

Christgau, Robert. "Patti Smith: Horses." http://www.robertchristgau.com/get_artist.php?name=Patti+Smith.

Cinquemani, Sal. "Patti Smith: Gung Ho." *SlantMagazine.com*. April 8, 2001. http://www.slantmagazine.com/music/review/patti-smith-gung-ho/173.

Clairedelune49. "Patti Smith the Boy the Beast and the Butterfly Poetry Project Marathon 2010." https://www.youtube.com/watch?v=wbmzZc0A4YM. Great example of Smith performing a poem as opposed to a song.

"The Clinton Conversation." *Rolling Stone*. November 12, 1998. http://www.oceanstar.com/patti/intervus/981112rs.htm.

Conan, Neal. "Rocker Patti Smith, 'Dream of Life'" Podcast. National Public Radio. November 30, 2009. http://www.npr.org/templates/story/story.php?storyId=122059809.

Cott, Jonathan. "Rock and Rimbaud." *New York Times*. February 19, 1978: 9, 29.

Creative Mornings. "Luis Resto: From Patti Smith to Eminem." August 8, 2013. https://www.youtube.com/watch?v=krELf1Pda-I.

Davis, Clive (author), and Anthony DeCurtis (collaborator). *The Soundtrack of My Life*. New York: Simon & Schuster, 2012: 220–31.

Davis, Stephen. "They Speak for Their Generation." *New York Times*. December 21, 1975: 119.

Delano, Sharon. "The Torch Singer." *New Yorker*. March 11, 2002. http://www.newyorker.com/archive/2002/03/11/020311fa_fact_delano.

Dream of Life . Dir. Steven Sebring. Palm Pictures. 2007. DVD. Documentary film shows a lot of candid moments including life on the road and a visit with Smith's parents.

Empire, Kitty. "Patti Smith: Banga—Review. *The Guardian*. June 2, 2012. http://www.theguardian.com/music/2012/jun/03/patti-smith-banga-review.

"Flashes." *Spin*. September 1986: 16.

Fleming, Mike, Jr.. "John Logan and Patti Smith Duet on Her Robert Mapplethorpe Memoir 'Just Kids.'" *Deadline Hollywood*. August 15, 2011. http://www.deadline.com/2011/08/john-logan-duets-with-patti-smith-on-just-kids/.

Foehr, Steven. "Death and the Rebirth of Patti Smith." *Shambhala Sun*. July 1996. Web.http://www.shambhalasun.com/index.php?option=com_content&task=view&id=2080.

"Fred Smith's Obituary from the Village Voice." http://www.oceanstar.com/patti/bio/fredobit.htm

Fricke, David. "Patti Smith: Family Life, Recent Loss, and New Album 'Gone Again.'" *Rolling Stone*. July 11, 1996. http://www.rollingstone.com/music/news/the-rolling-stone-interview-patti-smith-19960711.

———. "Patti Smith: Gone Again." *Rolling Stone*. December 2, 1996. http://www.rollingstone.com/music/albumreviews/gone-again-19961202.

———. "Patti Smith: Land." *Rolling Stone*. March 20, 2002. http://www.rollingstone.com/music/albumreviews/land-1975-2002-20020320.

———. "Patti Smith on Blake and Bush." *Rolling Stone*. May 5, 2004. http://www.rollingstone.com/music/news/patti-smith-on-blake-and-bush-20040505.

———. "Patti Smith: Peace and Noise." *Rolling Stone*. October 6, 1997. http://www.rollingstone.com/music/albumreviews/peace-and-noise-19971006.

Frith, Simon. "Review of Wave." *Melody Maker*. May 5, 1979. http://www.oceanstar.com/patti/crit/79frith.htm.

Gianni, Melissa. "Patti Smith on When to Break Rules and Nap on Logs." *Spin*. May 24, 2012. http://www.spin.com/articles/patti-smith-when-break-rules-and-nap-logs/.

Graff, Gary. "Patti Smith Recorded 'An Unexpected Gift' for Amy Winehouse." *Billboard*. May 30, 2012. http://www.billboard.com/articles/news/485475/patti-smith-recorded-an-unexpected-gift-for-amy-winehouse.

Green, Penny. "Interview with Patti Smith." *Interview*. October 1973. http://www.oceanstar.com/patti/intervus/730000in.htm. Early interview showcases Smith's early ideas and insights on performing, poetry, and music.

Grigoriadis, Vanessa. "Remembrances of the Punk Prose Poetess." *New York Magazine.* January 18, 2010. http://nymag.com/arts/music/profiles/63035/.

Gross, Amy. "Introducing Rock 'n' Roll's Lady Raunch." *Mademoiselle.* September 1975. http://www.oceanstar.com/patti/intervus/7509made.htm.

———. "'Just Kids': Punk Icon Patti Smith Looks Back." Podcast. National Public Radio. January 19, 2010. http://www.npr.org/templates/story/story.php?storyId=122722618.

Grossman, Pamela. "Eddie Vedder, Patti Smith Go Green at NYC Nader Rally." *Rolling Stone.* October 16, 2000. http://www.rollingstone.com/music/news/eddie-vedder-patti-smith-go-green-at-nyc-nader-rally-20001016.

Hand, Elizabeth. "Book Review: 'Just Kids' by Patti Smith." *Washington Post.* January 26, 2010. http://www.washingtonpost.com/wp-dyn/content/article/2010/01/25/AR2010012503700.html.

Hiss, Tony, and David McClelland. "Patti 'n' the Record Biz." *New York Times Magazine.* December 21, 1975. http://www.oceanstar.com/patti/intervus /751221ny.htm.

HistoireDuRockEnVidéos Patti Smith. "Patti Smith—7 Ways of Going—1979—Rockpalast." November 18, 2012. https://www.youtube.com/watch?v=n9tunZLhvKo. Excellent example of Smith's clarinet playing and improvisatory methods.

Hobbs, Mary Anne. "Patti Smith and Darren Aronofsky." *BBC Radio.* April 5, 2014. http://www.bbc.co.uk/programmes/b03zxbk1.

Holden, Stephen. "Patti Smith Returns with Motherly Wisdom." *New York Times.* July 28, 1988. http://articles.chicagotribune.com/1988-07-28/features/8801180200_1_patti-smith-fred-smith-child.

Horning, Rob. "Patti Smith: Trampin'" May 26, 2004. http://www.popmatters.com/review/smithpatti-trampin/.

Houston, Rita. "Patti Smith Explores the Classics." National Public Radio. June 21, 2007. http://www.npr.org/templates/story/story.php?storyId=10345784.

Howard, David N. *Sonic Alchemy: Visionary Music Producers and Their Maverick Recordings.* Milwaukee, WI: Hal Leonard, 2004: 193–94.

"In Damnation of . . . Horses by Patti Smith." *Flaming Pablum.* July 20, 2005. http://vassifer.blogs.com/alexinnyc/2005/07/in_damnation_of.html.

"Inside Music: Interviews / Patti Smith." April 24, 2007. http://entertainment.msn.com/news/article.aspx?news=259585.

Isler, Scott. "Patti Smith Defies Death." *Newsday.* June 23, 1996. http://www.oceanstar.com/patti/crit/ganewsda.htm.

Itzkoff, Dave. "Ain't It Strange: Patti Smith on her 'Law & Order' Experience." *New York Times.* June 20, 2011. http://artsbeat.blogs.nytimes.com/2011/06/20/aint-it-strange-patti-smith-on-her-law-order-experience/?_php=true&_type=blogs&_r=0.

Jefferson, Margo. "Touch of the Poet." *Newsweek.* December 29, 1975. http://www.oceanstar.com/patti/intervus/751229nw.htm.

Johnstone, Nick. *Patti Smith: A Biography.* New York: Omnibus Press, 1997. The first comprehensive biography on Patti that beautifully captures her life and career up until her second comeback.

Jones, Chris. "Patti Smith Trampin' Review." 2004. http://www.bbc.co.uk/music/reviews/mbmq.

Kern, Kevin. "Revisiting a Sophomore 'Slump.'" June 15, 2011. http://popstache.com/features/old-stache/revisiting-a-sophomore-slump/

King, Greg. "Songs of Experience: Patti Smith's Journey from Rock Singer to Mother to Radical Icon." *Sun Magazine.* July 2005: 4–7.

Klein, Joshua. "Patti Smith: Twelve." *Pitchfork Media.* April 20, 2007. http://pitchfork.com/reviews/albums/10137-twelve/.

Kornelis, Chris. "Q&A: Patti Smith on Robert Mapplethorpe, Jesus Christ, Poetry vs. Lyrics, and the Death of Kurt Cobain." *Seattle Weekly.* January 19, 2010. http://www.seattleweekly.com/home/926553-129/interview.

Kot, Greg. "Patti Smith Peace and Noise." *Chicago Tribune.* October 17, 1997. http://articles.chicagotribune.com/1997-10-17/entertainment/9710170108_1_sound-patti-smith-peace-and-noise.

La Gorce, Tammy. "Music; Patti Smith, New Jersey's Truest Rock-Poet." *New York Times.* December 11, 2005. http://query.nytimes.com/gst/fullpage.html?res=950CE0D81031F932A25751C1A9639C8B63.

Lane, Mary M. "How Katniss Everdeen Inspired Rocker Patti Smith." *Wall Street Journal.* June 20, 2012. http://blogs.wsj.com/speakeasy/2012/06/20/how-katniss-everdeen-inspired-rocker-patti-smith/.

Lanham, Tom. "Patti Smith—Trampin'" *Paste.* June 1, 2004. http://www.pastemagazine.com/articles/2004/06/patti-smith-trampin.html.

Litt, Anne. "Patti Smith: Morning Becomes Eclectic." November 15, 2012. http://www.kcrw.com/music/programs/mb/mb121115patti_smith.

Manson, Shirley. "100 Greatest Artists: Patti Smith." *Rolling Stone.* 2004. http://www.rollingstone.com/music/lists/100-greatest-artists-of-all-time-19691231/patti-smith-20110420.

Marren, David. "Patti Smith—Banga—Album Review." June 9, 2012. http://louderthanwar.com/patti-smith-banga-album-review/.

Marsh, Dave. "Patti Smith: Easter Review." *Rolling Stone.* April 10, 1978. http://www.rollingstone.com/music/albumreviews/easter-19780420.

———. "Review of Radio Ethiopia," *Rolling Stone.* January 13, 1977. http://www.rollingstone.com/music/albumreviews/radio-ethiopia-19770113.

McDonnell, Evelyn. "Because the Night." *The Village Voice.* August 1, 1995. http://www.oceanstar.com/patti/intervus/950801vv.htm.

———. "Patti Smith's 'Banga.'" *Los Angeles Times.* June 4, 2012. http://latimesblogs.latimes.com/music_blog/2012/06/album-review-patti-smiths-banga.html.

McLane, Daisann. "Power of Babble." *Crawdaddy.* May 1978. http://www.oceanstar.com/patti/crit/7805craw.htm.

McLean, Craig. "Patti Smith: 'I'm More Worried about the Death of a Bee Than I Am about Terrorism.'" *Telegraph.* June 6, 2012. http://www.telegraph.co.uk/culture/music/rockandpopfeatures/9300370/Patti-Smith-Im-more-worried-about-the-death-of-a-bee-than-I-am-about-terrorism.html.

McNeil, Legs, and Gillian McCain. *Please Kill Me: The Uncensored Oral History of Punk.* New York: Grove Press, 1996. Excellent offering on the early days of CBGB and the punk rock movement as a whole.

"Michael Stipe." http://www.oceanstar.com/patti/bio/stipe.htm.

Milzoff, Rebecca. "Influences: Patti Smith." *New York Magazine.* December 2, 2005. http://nymag.com/nymetro/arts/music/pop/15172/.

Moore, Thurston. "Interview with Patti Smith." *Bomb.* Winter 1996: 50–53.

Morrisroe, Patricia. *Mapplethorpe: A Biography.* Random House, 1995: 224–25, 229.

Myers, Paul. *A Wizard, a True Star: Todd Rundgren in the Studio.* London: Jawbone Press, 2010: 183–96.

Newlin, Jimmy. "Patti Smith: Twelve." *Slant.* April 23, 2007. http://www.slantmagazine.com/music/review/patti-smith-twelve/1097.

Newman, Melinda. "Arista's Smith Is Back With 'Gone.'" *Billboard.* June 8, 1996.

NJParlez. "Ivan Kral 1986 Interview." December 23, 2011. https://www.youtube.com/watch?v=inWQwYQX2Aw.

O'Brien, Lucy. *She Bop: The Definitive History of Women in Rock, Pop & Soul.* New York: Penguin Books, 1995: 111–17.

O'Hagan, Sean. "Michael Stipe: 'I Often Find Myself at a Loss for Words.'" *The Guardian.* March 5, 2011. http://www.theguardian.com/music/2011/mar/06/michael-stipe-rem-collapse-interview.

Paglia, Camille. *Sex, Art and American Culture.* New York: Random House, 1992.

Palmer, Robert. "Dream of Life." *Rolling Stone.* August 25, 1988. http://www.rollingstone.com/music/albumreviews/dream-of-life-19880825.

Pareles, Jon. "Fans of a Groundbreaking Club Mourn and Then Move On." *New York Times.* October 16, 2006. http://www.nytimes.com/2006/10/16/arts/music/16cnd-cbgbnotebook.html.

————. "RECORDINGS: A Trio of Wild-Eyed Rebels Try Comebacks." *New York Times*. July 10, 1988. http://www.nytimes.com/1988/07/10/arts/recordings-a-trio-of-wild-eyed-rebels-try-comebacks.html.

Partridge, Marianne. "Review of Radio Ethiopia." *Melody Maker*. October 23, 1976. http://www.oceanstar.com/patti/crit/7610melo.htm.

"Patti Smith Looks Ahead to New Projects after 'Banga.'" *Rolling Stone*. June 19, 2012. http://www.rollingstone.com/music/news/patti-smith-looks-ahead-to- new-projects-after-banga-20120619.

"Patti Smith Reflects on Power of Words, Rock 'n' Roll." December 29, 2010. http://www.pbs.org/newshour/bb/entertainment-july-dec10-pattismith_12-29/.

"Patti Smith Says New CBGBs Movie 'Seems Ridiculous." June 7, 2012. http://theinterro-bang.com/2012/06/patti-smith-says-new-cbgbs-movie-seems-ridiculous/.

"Patti Smith to Narrate Tubby the Tuba with Little Orchestra Society, 3/16." January 3, 2013. http://www.broadwayworld.com/article/Patti-Smith-to-Narrate-TUBBY-THE-TUBA-with-Little-Orchestra-Society-316-20130103.

"Patti Smith: Twelve." *Billboard*. April 28, 2007.

Patti Smith: Under Review. 2008. DVD. Documentary film.

"Patti Smith Wins Polar Music Prize." *NME*. August 30, 2011. http://www.nme.com/news/patti-smith/58939.

PEN America. "Patti Smith and Jonathan Lethem in Conversation." May 4, 2010. Video offers stunning insights on how Smith feels about modern-day New York City. https://www.youtube.com/watch?v=0cHL-VXYSgI.

Penner, John. "The Patti Smith Group 'Radio Ethiopia' (1976); Arista." *Los Angeles Times*. December 12, 1992. http://articles.latimes.com/1992-12-17/news/ol-2857_1_radio-ethiopia.

Pennington, Zac. "Radio Fort Lauderdale: Relevance vs. Patti Smith." *Portland Mercury*. August 12, 2004. http://www.portlandmercury.com/portland/radio-fort-lauderdale/Content?oid=31901.

Penny, Jenn. "Patti Smith Planning Sequel to Just Kids." *Pitchfork Media*. December 18, 2012. http://pitchfork.com/news/48978-patti-smith-planning-sequel-to-just-kids/.

Phipps, Keith. "Patti Smith: Gung Ho." *The AV Club*. March 21, 2000. http://www.avclub.com/review/patti-smith-emgung-hoem-21684.

Postingoldtapes. "Patti Smith on Talk Show Promoting Her Book *Babel*." July 7, 2010. https://www.youtube.com/watch?v=9N5beZ_CCXk.

"Premiere: Patti Smith on New 'After the Gold Rush' Cover." *Rolling Stone*. June 4, 2012. http://www.rollingstone.com/music/videos/premiere-patti-smith-on-new-after-the-gold-rush-cover-20120604.

Punk: Attitude. Dir. Don Letts. Shout! Factory. 2005. DVD. Documentary film.

Reynolds, Simon. "Even as a Child, I Felt like an Alien." *The Observer*. May 21, 2005. http://www.theguardian.com/music/2005/may/22/popandrock1.

Rigi, Len. "Patti Smith Still Uncovering Reasons behind 'Twelve' Covers Disc." *Popmatters*. August 2, 2007. http://www.popmatters.com/article/patti-smith-still-uncovering-reasons-behind-twelve-covers-disc/.

Robinson, Lisa. "Patti Smith Talks about Radio Ethiopia." *Hit Parader*. Summer-fall 1977. http://www.oceanstar.com/patti/intervus/770700hp.htm.

Rock and Roll Hall of Fame + Museum. "Patti Smith Accepts Award Rock and Roll Hall of Fame Inductions 2007." January 21, 2011. https://www.youtube.com/watch?v=wep1sSO-umw. Video of Patti's acceptance speech shows her humility and grace.

————. "Zack De La Rocha Inducts Patti Smith Rock and Roll Hall of Fame Inductions 2007." January 21, 2011. https://www.youtube.com/watch?v=-dj5Rr7tYzI.

Rockwell, John. "Patti Smith Battles to a Singing Victory." *New York Times*. December 28, 1975: 31.

————. "Patti Smith: Horses." *Rolling Stone*. February 12, 1976. http://www.rollingstone.com/music/albumreviews/horses-19760212.

RollingStones50yrs1. "Patti Smith—Horses (Old Grey Whistle Test, 1976)." November 6, 1976. https://www.youtube.com/watch?v=8egNoThqJng.

Sandlin, Michael. "Patti Smith: Gung Ho." *Pitchfork Media*. March 21, 2000. http://pitchfork.com/reviews/albums/7275-gung-ho/.

Saturday Night Live. NBC. December 9, 1978. DVD.

———. NBC. February 17, 1979. DVD.

Scelsa, Vin. "Dream of Life." *Penthouse*. October 1988. http://www.oceanstar.com/patti/crit/8810pent.htm.

Schaefer, John. "John Schaefer Talks to Patti Smith about New 'Banga' Album." *WNYC*. June 10, 2012. http://www.wnyc.org/story/215269-john-schaefer-talks-patti-smith-about-her-new-banga-album/.

Schmeig, Sam. "Luis Resto Discusses His Musical Roots, Writing with Eminem & Studio Vibes." November 22, 2013. http://www.closedsessions.com/tag/luis-resto/.

Schwartz, Andy. "Patti Smith—A Wave Hello, a Kiss Goodbye." *New York Rocker*. June/July 1979. http://www.oceanstar.com/patti/intervus/7906nyr.htm.

Shapiro, Susan. "Patti Smith: Somewhere over the Rimbaud." *Crawdaddy*. December 1975. http://www.oceanstar.com/patti/intervus/7512craw.htm.

Smith, Kimberly. "Beverly Williams Smith Tribute." March 18, 2013. https://www.youtube.com/watch?v=euqNbKcZhHA.

Smith, Patti. "Banga." May 29, 2012. https://www.youtube.com/watch?v=8cbmS0IfBjQ.

———. "Jukebox Cruci-fix." *Creem*. June 1975. http://www.oceanstar.com/patti/poetry/jukebox.htm.

———. *Just Kids*. New York: HarperCollins, 2010: 3–88, 265–79.

———. "Lou Reed." *The New Yorker*. November 11, 2013. http://www.newyorker.com/talk/2013/11/11/131111ta_talk_smith.

———. "'Lou Reed Was a Very Special Poet.'" *Rolling Stone*. October 28, 2013. http://www.rollingstone.com/music/news/patti-smith-lou-reed-was-a-very-special-poet-20131028.

———. "Nine (from 'Banga')." June 8, 2012. https://www.youtube.com/watch?v=MMxCb6DiDbE&list=PL8F7A8A64BFB75505.

———. "Off the Shelf." *The New Yorker*. October 10, 2011. http://www.newyorker.com/reporting/2011/10/10/111010fa_fact_smith.

———. *Patti Smith Complete 1975–2006: Lyrics, reflections and notes for the future*. New York: HarperCollins, 2006: 18–27, 30, 32, 40, 65, 66, 85, 96, 100, 138, 145, 154, 167, 174, 180, 184, 185, 204, 227, 243, 249, 280. Features all of her lyrics until 2006 as well as journal notes and brief insights into her musical output.

Smith, Patti. "Television: 'Somewhere Somebody Must Stand Naked.'" October 1974: 21. http://www.rockscenester.com/rockscene09book/.

South Bank Show. ITV. April 1, 1978. DVD.

Stipe, Michael. *Two Times Intro: On the Road with Patti Smith*. Brooklyn, NY: Akashic Books, 2011: preface.

Strauss, Neil. "Patti Smith, Surrounded by Ghosts, Still Rocks." *New York Times*. June 24, 1996. http://www.nytimes.com/1996/06/24/arts/pop-review-patti-smith-surrounded-by-ghosts-still-rocks.html.

Strombo. "Patti Smith: Extended Interview on George Stroumboulopoulos Tonight." March 12, 2013. https://www.youtube.com/watch?v=pvZ2MwB2vvs. Excellent interview where Smith discusses her early life and upbringing.

Sutton, Benjamin. "Patti Smith Talks to Jonathan Lethem, Tells Aspiring Artists to Find New City." *The L Magazine*. May 4, 2010. http://www.thelmagazine.com/TheMeasure/archives/2010/05/04/patti-smith-talks-to-jonathan-lethem-tells-aspiring-artists-to-find-new-city.

TheNYeye. "Pratt Commencement 2010—Patti Smith—Keynote Speaker." July 8, 2010. https://www.youtube.com/watch?v=ZJjc1ARnwY8.

Tom51. "Patti Smith Interviewed by Tom Snyder." February 23, 2009. https://www.youtube.com/watch?v=iNg19CH9AwY.

Tosches, Nick. "Review of Easter." *Creem*. June 1978. http://www.oceanstar.com/patti/crit/tosches.htm.

Tucker, Ken. "On 'Banga,' Patti Smith Pays Homage to Friends." National Public Radio. June 14, 2012. http://www.npr.org/2012/06/14/155014549/on-banga-patti-smith-pays-homage-to-friends.

Tulifuli. "Allen Ginsberg Memorial Patti Smith Tuli Kupferberg Paint It Red & Black." April 5, 2011. https://www.youtube.com/watch?v=JXXUcChoZ0g.

Ulin, David. "Patti Smith's Woolgathering." *Los Angeles Times*. December 25, 2011. http://articles.latimes.com/2011/dec/25/entertainment/la-ca-patti-smith-20111225.

Vinciquerra, Lisa. "Patti Smith Inducts Velvet Underground Rock and Roll Hall of Fame 1996." December 8, 2011. https://www.youtube.com/watch?v=US4X92vdbQ4.

Vulliamy, Ed. "Some Give a Song. Some Give a Life . . ." *The Guardian*. June 2, 2005. http://www.theguardian.com/music/2005/jun/03/meltdownfestival2005.meltdownfestival.

WENN. "Patti Smith Blames Crew for Stage Plunge." *Contactmusic.com*. May 23, 2012. http://www.contactmusic.com/news/patti-smith-blames-crew-for-stage-plunge_1332027.

———. "Patti Smith—Patti Smith Dedicates Song to Edward Snowden and Russian Punk Rockers." *Contactmusic.com*. January 2, 2014. http://www.contactmusic.com/story/patti-smith-dedicates-song-to-edward-snowden-and-russian-punk-rockers_4008976.

Whittaker, Jason. "Innocent Augur—Patti Smith's Blake." April 2, 2010. http://zoamorphosis.com/2010/04/innocent-augur-patti-smiths-blake/.

Young, Charles M. "Visions of Patti." *Rolling Stone*. July 27, 1978. http://www.oceanstar.com/patti/crit/rs780727.htm.

FURTHER LISTENING

SINGLES: MER RECORDS

"Piss Factory / Hey Joe"

1974. Patti's first foray into recording showcases her primal use of juxtaposing rock and roll and poetry, utilizing only voice, guitar, and piano. Patti's barebones instrumentation allows for her vocals and lyrical style to be the focal point without much distraction. On "Piss Factory," Patti's detailed account of factory life is easily transmitted with aid from the piano's jazzy influence. Patti's take on "Hey Joe" relies heavily on improvisation from the guitar, adding tension and release in the otherwise close assembly of instruments.

ALBUMS: ARISTA RECORDS

Horses

December 13, 1975. Smith's debut album elevated Patti from the provincial scene at CBGB to the national stage. In an era where top-40 starlets are seen as mere sexual objects, Smith's androgynous look, aided by the stunning cover photo taken by Robert Mapplethorpe, redefined the concept of female-fronted rock and roll. Smith's interpretation of the Van Morrison penned song "Gloria" was heralded for its subversive opening line "Jesus died for somebody's sins but not mine," and it has since became a staple of Smith's catalog.

Radio Ethiopia

October 1976. For their follow-up record, Patti and Co. enlisted the help of producer Jack Douglas in hopes of appealing to a larger fan base. The resulting work was panned, with many calling attention to the album's title track being aimless and a failed experiment of rock-and-roll improvisation. Songs such as "Ask the Angels" and "Pumping (My Heart)" show the band's intent for a hit single while remaining true to its art. Subsequent reviews and readings of the album are more favorable, with many believing that the negative attention came from the fact that the group had the difficult task of living up to the initial success of *Horses*.

Easter

March 3, 1978. With the stench of the sophomore slump-viewed *Radio Ethiopia* behind them, Patti and the band crafted a variety of songs for *Easter* that ran along a diverse musical palette. Most noteworthy is "Because the Night," a song cowritten by Bruce Springsteen that became the group's first top-20 single. Additionally, the album proved controversial with the song "Rock and Roll Nigger," a blistering rock song that reclaimed the use of the word "nigger" as a way of describing someone on the outskirts of society.

Wave

May 17, 1979. Riding a surge of popularity due to the success of "Because the Night," the band enlisted the help of musician/producer Todd Rundgren. The resulting batch of songs featured a more radio-compatible and mainstream sound than its previous efforts. During this time, Smith began to feel disenchanted with rock stardom, which is overtly heard on her take of the song "So You Want to Be a Rock 'n' Roll Star?" This would be Patti's last album before taking a nine-year sabbatical.

Dream of Life

June 1988. After being away from the spotlight for the better part of a decade, Smith's comeback record was eagerly anticipated by both critics and the public. The album is most notable for her collaboration with her husband, Fred "Sonic" Smith, who served as cowriter, coproducer, and guitarist. Amid songs about love, motherhood, and politics, the overall sound has a mainstream and explicit aural tendency. However, a lack of touring on the part of Smith, having given birth around the time of the record's release, ultimately sank its commercial prospects. The album's first single, "People Have the Power," lived on as a bona fide political anthem, with Green Party candidate and presidential hopeful Ralph Nader using the song during political events.

Gone Again

June 18, 1996. After *Dream of Life* failed to bring her back to the mainstream, Patti returned with an album steeped in heartbreak and grief. After losing her husband, Fred, as well as Robert Mapplethorpe, Richard Sohl, and her brother Todd, Patti channeled her despair into a series of songs that represent the rhythm of life. With "Gone Again" and "Summer Cannibals," Patti channels her energies with saturated mid-1990s rock textures, while utilizing country qualities on "Wing" and "Ravens." Patti's inclusion of Bob Dylan's "Wicked Messenger" adds a much-needed, sultry, blues-inspired romp on an album sharp with melancholy.

Peace and Noise

September 30, 1997. While the aura of death that *Gone Again* skillfully executed is still prevalent on *Peace and Noise* (with song titles such as "Death Singing," "Dead City," and "Memento Mori"), Patti uses a more eclectic lyrical palette to speak about death. On "Waiting Underground," Smith speaks of loss, not through despair, but through anger over the losses that she has incurred throughout her life. "Whirl Away" juxtaposes the serious subject of the fragility of life against a reggae-infused background. *Peace and Noise* also warranted Patti her first Grammy Award nomination for the song "1959."

Gung Ho

March 21, 2000. Patti tackles political and religious issues in the face of a post–Bill Clinton time in American society with *Gung Ho*. With songs about Mother Theresa ("One Voice") and Salome ("Lo and Beholden"), Patti's religious inclination is in the forefront at the dawn of the new millennium. *Gung Ho* features Patti at her most lyrically overt, with her condemning the monetary stronghold of youth ("Glitter in Their Eyes") and the disapproval of imperialism ("Gung Ho").

Land: 1975–2002

March 19, 2002. Part greatest-hits package, part rarities collection, and part live album, *Land 1975–2002* compiles the most noteworthy songs in Patti's catalog with a bent toward her early material. The addition of early demos of "Redondo Beach" and "Distant Fingers" shows the evolution of the respective songs and the Patti Smith Group as a unit. Live versions of some of her latter-day material, such as "Wing" and "Boy Cried Wolf," demonstrate how time has only served to make Patti that much stronger a performer.

ALBUMS: COLUMBIA RECORDS

Trampin'

April 27, 2004. With her first record for Columbia Records after twenty-seven years with Arista Records, Patti and Co. serve a set of politically saturated songs. Given the post–September 11 time frame that the album was released, the songs never feel overly preachy but rather mature and thoughtful. While politics ring heavy on *Trampin'*, songs such as "Jubilee" and "Gandhi" examine spiritual and religious practices, while "Mother Rose" and "Cartwheel" parse the fragility of motherhood.

Twelve

April 17, 2007. While Patti has used covers as a ways of expressing her tastes, the series of covers chosen for *Twelve* plays out like a study in arranging and introducing established material to a new generation. *Twelve* is most successful when it completely reworks the genre of the original material. Patti's take on George Harrison's "Within You without You" replaces the sitar-infused psychedelic feel of the original with a softer acoustic palette. The highlight of the record is Patti's take on the classic grunge anthem "Smells like Teen Spirit," where she turns the original power-trio bravado of the original and replaces it with an acoustic ensemble, resulting in a temperamental, folksy feel.

Banga

June 1, 2012. Fresh off the success of her memoir *Just Kids*, Patti offers a varied thematic palette, with the title of the album coming from Russian author Mikhail Bulgakov's book *The Master and Margarita*. *Banga*'s output includes two eulogies ("Maria," "This Is the Girl"), a tome on sea exploration ("Amerigo"), and a song about the sheer destruction that Earth can surmise ("Fuji-San"), resulting in a diverse array of outlooks and styles.

INDEX

ABOUT THE AUTHOR

Eric Wendell is a New York–based musicologist. He earned his bachelor of music in music performance from Five Towns College, an master of arts in jazz history and research from Rutgers University, and a master of library science in library and information studies from Queens College. His writing has been featured in *Hot House Jazz Magazine*, Jazz.com, and *Music in American Life: An Encyclopedia of the Songs, Styles, Stars, and Stories That Shaped Our Culture*. As a musician, he has performed nationally with the band Trashed on Fiction and in select performances with several contemporary concert, jazz, and rock groups. He currently works as a librarian for a music publishing company in New York.